BRIDGING THE GAP

Life Lessons from the Dying

An Imprint of KCP Ventures/ Death by Design, LLC
Wilmington NC 28403

KCP Ventures offers this book in special quantity discounts for bulk purchases for sales promotions, premiums, fund-raising, and educational needs. Special books or book excerpts also can be crated to fit specific needs. For details, write Kimberly@deathbydesign.com.

Liberty of Congress Cataloging in process.

Name: Paul, Kimberly C.
Company: KCP Ventures, LLC (dba: Death by Design)
Title: Bridging The Gap: Life Lessons From The Dying / by Kimberly C. Paul
Description: Wilmington, NC: KCP Ventures, 2018 | Death by Design Product.
KCP Ventures, LLC Identifier: 01-00001-2018
Subjects: End Of Life | Terminal Care | Terminally ill – Care. | Hospice Care | Palliative Care
Medical Culture | Death | Design | Death by Design | Lessons From The Dying

Printed in the United States of America
10 9 8 7 6 5 4 3 2 1

Editors: Kimberly C. Paul, Hillary Hoggard, Quinn Cook, Beth Paul, and Ken Paul.

Book Design By Hillary Hoggard, Wilmington, NC

Book Cover Photos: Megan Deitz Photography (www.megandeitz.com) and Mary Jo Fish

Pictures Within Bridging The Gap: Jill Huckelberry, Megan Deitz Photography (www.megandeitz.com), Jon McLean, Jackson Thornton, Kenny Barnes and Kimberly C. Paul

Brief portions of this book have appeared on Death by Design's website and Thrive Global online media website.

BRIDGING THE GAP BETWEEN

Medical Culture ---------------- Community

Clinical ------------------------- Non-Clinical

Birth ------------------------------------ Death

Grief ------------------------------------ Living

Tears ------------------------------Happiness

LOVE

"The trouble is
you think you have time."

~Buddha

C850177 P5L

DISCLAIMER

I have tried to recreate events, locales and conversations from my memories of them. In order to maintain their anonymity in some instances I have changed the names of individuals and places, I may have changed some identifying characteristics and details such as physical properties, occupations and places of residence.

This book is not intended as a substitute for the medical advice of physicians. The reader should regularly consult a physician in matters relating to his/her health and particularly with respect to any symptoms that may require diagnosis or medical attention.

"You matter because you are you, and you matter to the last moment of your life. We will do all we can, not only to help you die peacefully, but also live until you die."

DAME CICELY SAUNDERS
NURSE, DOCTOR, SOCIAL WORKER AND WRITER
FOUNDER OF THE HOSPICE MOVEMENT (1918-2005)

GRATITUDE

To Apple
You're the reason. Thank you.

To My Parents
Thank you for your support and encouragement as I
left full-time employment to pursue my dream.

To All the Hospice Families and Patients
Thank you for opening up your lives to me, sharing your stories that have provided
the stepping stones and lessons so I could create a designed life around what
matters most.

To My Friends & Family
Thanks for understanding the long hours, the absent holidays and the lost moments
so I could breathe life into the stories within these pages.

To Haven
Thanks to my four-legged partner in crime who sat next to me, brainstormed in the
park with me, listened as I read out loud all the stories written over and over, who took
long walks with me to clear my head, reminded me to play and comforted me when I
cried writing many of the stories within these pages. Thank you for teaching me what
unconditional love is all about.

Teresa Fox
You've always believed in me. You've always supported me. You're my roots below the
tree that kept me grounded throughout this process. Thanks for the long conversations
and continued support on the dark days when no words would come.
You are my sister, cousin and part-time mom. Thank you!

Rebecca Peirce

Thank you for always challenging me and providing a different point of view. You did it with such grace and kindness. You're a great business advisor, and I'm so grateful you have been by my side on this new adventure.

Hillary Hoggard

You have brought color to my life. Your designs and viewpoint have helped my stories come alive. You are my sister.

To My Podcast Guests

Thank you for walking with me; teaching and mentoring me through the writing of this book. The conversations, the scheduling and planning it took to post a 30-minute interview about end of life on Death By Design's podcasts are much appreciated. It was an eventful journey. I am grateful for your company along the way.

To Garth Callaghan

Thank you for sending me a random email sharing the quote you wrote on a napkin note for your daughter. *"Many individuals worry about what they are about to leave behind, instead of focusing on what they are about to gain."* —Unknown
It changed my life. I do not believe I would be on this journey if it was not for you.

To G & E-Hay

You are family. Thank you so much for your friendship, love, support and, of course, Master Dixon. Your presence in my life is a true gift.

And thank you to ...

all the other individuals who sent me notes, read my blog, listened to my podcasts, and supported me in text messages and phone calls. You know who you are. I could not have done this without you nor would have I chosen this path. Thanks to my high school friends, to my youth group members at Winfree Memorial Baptist Church in Midlothian, Va., to my Angels from Meredith College in Raleigh, N.C., and to my friends in my hometown of Wilmington N.C., who often pulled me away from the computer to remind me to celebrate life.

Thank you ... Thank you... Thank you!

"If you experienced life through the eyes of a child, everything would be magical and extraordinary. Let our curiosity, adventure and wonder of life never end." -Akiane Kramarik

INTRODUCTION
In the beginning.

*"A little step may be the beginning of the
next great adventure."* —Unknown

I can't tell you how many times I've been asked, "How did you go from the hallways of "Saturday Night Live" and casting CBS daytime to hospice?" Obviously, there is a story behind my answer to that question.

My first exposure with death was my great grandmother's passing on my mother's side. Everyone in the family called her "Big Mamma." She was a tower of a woman, big not only in size but also in spirit. She worked for over 40 years at a Belk department store selling shoes. She ate cottage cheese with pineapple slices.

As a child, I was completely drawn to her. There was a history hidden behind her heart. I somehow related to the lessons and pain she must have felt as she weathered World War I and eventually saw her two sons join the army and head into battle during World War II.

She was very close to her two sisters, and one brother until they died. Her passing opened my eyes to a new experience. Death was a complete mystery to me before it became a career.

I remember it like it was yesterday. My brother, sister, and I were delivered to my father's parents' home for a few days as mom and dad discretely headed for the small, dying town of Ahoskie, N.C. There wasn't a lot of explanation about why we were going, but as kids we really didn't care. It was summer, and we had nothing but time.

We enjoyed several long hot days running around the open fields of our grandparents' 100-year-old farm. Chasing cows, destroying neatly stacked bales of hay in the barn, and speeding through the pastures on that dusty red go-cart, we were full of life without a thought about what the next few days would bring. It would be the last time I would recall this innocent feeling of being unaware that life is not as permanent as I once thought. I was 12.

As I laid my head to rest that last evening at the farm, I had a dream that would forever change my life. I actually envisioned Big Mamma's death. She came to me as I slept and explained that it was time for her to leave. She described the place where she was going as just another realm; full of positive energy and love. She told me to live boldly, embrace all moments whether happy or sad, and to always remember words from respectable elders who would cross my own path in life.

Before I knew it, I was awake and being told my great grandmother had passed on. When my mother told me she had died, I simply replied, "I know." I tried to explain the dream but was abruptly dismissed.

Searching for something to help me define how I felt about losing Big Mamma, I remembered that I had heard someone else speak of energy and reaching another realm. When I finally made the connection—I literally laughed out loud. It was the "Star Wars" series. You can laugh too, but the films took my young soul to another realm. The epic tales told an in-depth story about good and evil that is so similar to real life as we know it.

While watching the "The Empire Strikes Back," Luke Skywalker was being trained by his wise and respectable elder, Yoda. One scene in particular helped me connect the dots to discovering the meaning of positive energy and love.

Luke tried to raise his X-Wing fighter plane from the depths of a swamp. As Luke balanced himself upside down on one hand and Yoda stabilized on one of Luke's feet, he reached inside of himself to touch "the Force" to reclaim his X-Wing from the murky waters. Frustrated by only being able to lift rocks around the swamp, Yoda asked him to "feel the Force." Luke lost his concentration and he and Yoda collapsed to the ground.

"We'll never get it out now," Luke yelled as he walked to the edge of the swamp.

"So certain are you," Yoda said, shaking his head. "Always with you, what can't be done. Do you hear nothing what I say?"

"Master … moving stones is one thing. This …" Luke said as he pointed at the sunken ship, "… totally different."

"No, no different," Yoda said, shaking his head again. "Only different in your mind. You must unlearn what you have learned."

As Luke turned back to the ship he said, "Okay, I will give it a try."

"No, do not try," Yoda replied. "Do or do not. There is no try."

As Luke nodded and turned back to face the X-Wing, he closed his eyes and slightly raised the ship. It moved suddenly in the wrong direction, sinking it further into the depths of the dark swamp.

Yoda bowed his head in disappointment.

Exhaustion led to Luke's collapse next to Yoda as he turned to him and said, "I can't, it's too big."

"Size matter not," professed the wise elder. "Look at me. Judge me by my size, do you? And where you should not. 'The Force'—life creates it, makes it grow. Its energy surrounds us and between us. Luminous things are we. We are not this crude matter," as Yoda pointed to Luke's body. "You must feel 'the Force' around you, in you, between you … between me, the rock, everywhere and yes, even between the land and ship."

"You want the impossible!" Luke proclaimed as he stood up and walked away in his own discernment.

Yoda closed his eyes, and pointed his claw-like hand toward the X-Wing. The swamp began to bubble, then the ship magically started to rise and float toward the land as Luke watched in awe.

As Luke circled the ship, caressing it in all its glory and force, he said, "I don't believe it!"

"That is why you fail," said Yoda.

Why does this scene from the "Star Wars Trilogy" lead me to such a controversial subject as death? The answer is quite simple. It's a brilliant example of how one may be taught to think and how an empowering force can help one unlearn what they have been taught in order to expand to another realm of understanding.

This scene from "The Empire Strikes Back" helped me put my arms around death. I had to unlearn what I knew about death to embrace a new way of thinking about death. Death should not be perceived as taboo or a hard subject. Talking about death should be an engaging and light-hearted conversation. People are spiritual beings full of energy. Paraphrasing the eloquent words of Yoda, the wise and respectable elder, we are energy while we are breathing as well as far after our physical bodies have expired. Our energy moves beyond such crude matter … we are luminous beings.

I embrace the creative viewpoint that we can design a death that is transcendent. A death designed to open doors to an amazing experience that reflects our personal journey through life. If we have an opportunity to be creative and positive with the perceptual dark side of death, why not do it and do it well?

We must first birth a new way to think about our final chapters. If we dare, we can even design it. Thinking about our own deaths forces us to reflect on the life we are living both in the present and the past. Coming face to face with the lost moments scattered on the ground of my own life can be disheartening, but facing them makes me want to live more boldly in the last half of my life. If we face our wasted days and lost moments head on, we can embrace the life we choose to live with open arms.

In the following pages, I will share very rare and intimate moments at the bedside of dying patients who have taught me lessons that have changed me and enveloped me. Their experiences have allowed me to move far beyond my own downward glance at my shortcomings and to accept all the little things that make me completely, imperfectly … me.

Throughout my years working with the dying, I don't see death in any other way but color. Death is not black and white. Death is vibrant colors full of life, adventure, laughter, and hope. Designing your death requires thought, preparaton with legal documents, and communication, but mostly living in the present moment and embracing life to the fullest. I hope these stories inspire you to speak frankly, plan courageously and fully lean into the ultimate final adventure at the end of life.

BIG MOMMA, AUNT VIOLA, AUNT RUTH, UNCLE BOB

"She was very close to her two sisters, and one brother until they died. Her passing opened my eyes to a new experience. Death was a complete mystery to me before it became a career."

PREFACE

The stories in Bridging The Gap have nothing to do with death, but everything to do with all the days in between birth and death. These stories show ordinary individuals making extraordinary choices, inspiring others to take action in end of life planning. But mostly these stories are encouragement to participate in life and to design a life around what matters most and not just allow death to be a final destination. This book is about the days lived prior to taking our last breath that could radically change how we die, how our loved ones grieve us, and even how the medical culture serves us. Each story is based upon true events that have occurred in my life and during my time working in hospice care. It is about life and living … until the moment it ends.

CONTENTS

"Content is the reason search began." ~Unknown

"To the well-organized mind, death is but the next great adventure." —J.K. Rowling

CHAPTER ONE

Life Lesson: Miracles happen every day.

"Miracles happen every day. Not just in remote country villages or at holy sites halfway across the globe, but here, in our own lives."
—Deepak Chopra

In late 2016, I was on the verge of celebrating my 17th year in hospice care. I found myself sitting at my desk staring out the window toward the wooded area beyond our hospice parking lot. I had just recovered from pneumonia and was struggling to regain my momentum with work. Something was missing, but I didn't know what or how to change that fact. I was afraid, and fear of failure paralyzed me. I didn't know who I was without my beloved hospice organization, but something needed to change. I just didn't know what or how to make the change.

Moments prior to my weekly meeting with our new CEO, I received a note from Garth Callaghan. It was written on a napkin and simply read, "One reason people resist change is because they focus on what they have to give up instead of on what they have to gain." I knew then it was time to leave the job I loved.

Thirty days later, I resigned, cashed in my retirement, and began working on my podcast and book project. I never looked back, because I knew in my heart it was time to go. I did not want to resist the change and be afraid of what I was giving up. I wanted to open myself up to new adventures that could lead to all the things I might gain by leaving the

9-5 world behind. I knew I could continue my vision of end of life education by creating Death by Design and finally live the life so many hospice patients had taught me how to live. I chose to no longer rush through life, but to walk and stop to take notice of the simple pleasures.

Launching Death by Design Podcast in January 2017 gave me the opportunity to meet New York Times best-selling authors, get to know my neighbors, and learn from people making small differences in their own communities as they added to the larger drumbeat that was becoming the cadence for end of life discussions. I met individuals who shared their personal stories and heard caregivers' stories. I was introduced to physicians changed by their own personal experiences and saw artists trying to normalize the subject of death and dying.

I came across people like Garth Callaghan who, through his heart-felt napkin notes written to a daughter from a dying father, ended up touching my life too. It was in his encouraging napkin note addressed to me that I found the strength to take my own leap of faith and leave full-time employment. His words were a small miracle in my life.

Miracles happen every day, but we are too busy to see them. So many times, people forget to ask for what they want or need, because they feel too vulnerable or think they are setting themselves up for disappointment. There are so many life lessons I've learned over the years that I would have never experienced if I had not been awake throughout my journey. I'm so grateful that I took notice of so many individuals. Their stories changed how I have chosen to live and how I will choose to die.

LESSONS I HAVE LEARNED

Miracles happen every day.

No one talks about death. Connection and communication are why we are alive.

It is the simple things that matter most.

Death is universal and will touch us all.

Advocating for others opens your heart to love.

Forgiveness is key to happiness.

Unconditional love can change the world.

Always ask for what you want, because you just might get it.

Wisdom trumps education.

Life is a mystery. Stop trying to figure it out and just accept it as fact.

Physicians are not God, they're human just like you and me.

Change your perspective, and it will change your life.

Trust your gut. It is the best compass we have.

Closure is a myth.

Be authentic … just be.

There are many more life lessons I learned throughout my year, and I continue to learn each day. Working in hospice care made me acutely aware that life is fragile and short. I am forever grateful for every lesson I have learned at the bedside of friends who just happen to be dying.

"Life is a brief intermission, between
birth and death, enjoy it." —Unknown

CHAPTER TWO

Life Lesson: Connection and communication are why we are alive.

"The key to communication is connection." —Unknown

I was slowly recovering from the end of a relationship and was not yet aware of how that chapter of my life would eventually unfold. The year was 1999, and just like Prince recommended, I partied like it was too.

I was illogically trying to plug the pain of a lost relationship with another relationship. It wasn't the brightest idea. I thought by leaving New York City I would find a community again, but I was grasping at anything that walked past me to keep my chin above water; just trying to stay afloat.

Choosing to relocate to Wilmington, N.C., I was hoping to work in the film and television industry once more. Wilmington was known as the "Hollywood of the East" at the time, and I had high hopes for being in the south, living a creative life and enjoying the sea breeze from the Atlantic Ocean on a daily basis. When I arrived, however, the one big show, "Dawson's Creek" was on hiatus. The good ol' boy network wasn't very impressed with my major credits from New York City. I needed a job, and I needed one quick.

I had obtained my degree in social work. Believe me, there is nothing social about that line of work, but I was hoping it would open some doors to a few non-profit jobs in the growing coastal town. I started to apply. I had several interviews, but "ho-spice" was the first offer I received. (I was new to the healthcare world and language. Being very green within the industry, I naively referred to hospice as "ho·spice".) The position included managing volunteers who provided "ho·spice" to families in five counties with respite care and other vital needs. It also required assisting the marketing and communications departments when needed.

I took the job and was quickly schooled by one of the senior nurses that "ho·spice" was actually pronounced hospice. I knew then my learning curve would be severe, but I assumed it would be nothing like what it had been working on live network television shows in New York.

What was interesting to me about hospice was that everyone seemed to have a personal story about life, love, death, and loss. I loved a good story, especially ones that included those subject matters.

On my first official day after orientation, I was assigned to ride with one of the chaplains. Jim seemed nice, but by the way he looked at me, I knew he was questioning my young age and credentials. Before starting out, I received a 1·0·1 on the "do's and don'ts" of hospice. I'll just say the list weighed heavily on the "don'ts," and literally made me sweat.

The Do List: Listen. Observe.

The Don't List: Talk. Stare. Engage. Accept gifts. Open your mouth. Ask to go to the bathroom. Ask for food or water. Make eye contact. Acknowledge odors.

"Odors?" I asked.

"Odors," he confirmed without even looking at me.

I was getting the feeling that my presence was a forced and unwelcomed assignment for him. I just took notes and was thrilled that I had a job. I was used to being ordered around and not speaking a lot anyway.

Arriving at the first patient's house, I was nervous. I had never talked or listened to someone who was knowingly dying. I wondered what it would be like to have an open conversation about the end, God, and life.

As we exited the car, Jim had one last instruction for me. "Stay behind me and don't speak." I just nodded my head. Suddenly, a herd of individuals abruptly pushed their way through the screen door and intercepted us on the front lawn.

"Good morning," Jim said with softness. His voice sounded so kind and sweet and his voice had an entirely different tone than I had heard in his strict instructions delivered to me just minutes before we arrived.

"My sisters and brothers wanted to talk to you prior to visiting our mother," said a tall, slender gentleman in his early 60s. He looked tired and worried.

"Sure," Jim replied.

"We don't want you to tell our mother she is dying," another younger sibling chimed in. "We don't think she would be able to handle the situation."

I didn't say a word. I felt confused and raised my eyebrows at the situation. Weren't you supposed to know you were dying when ho-spice, I mean hospice, was called in to your home? Still not uttering a word, I made a mental note to ask Jim that very question after the visit.

"I assure you, we will not talk about anything your mother does not bring up," Jim said. I was surprised at his response. "We are here to listen and support."

The faces of the children seemed to relax, and they allowed us to continue into the house. Halfway up the stairs, I heard a loud, distinct Yankee accent call out, "Who's there? Hurry up and get up here!"

Without hesitation, Jim and I picked up our pace. Though the door was open, Jim knocked and asked the elderly woman if we could enter.

"Of course. Who do you think I've been talking to?" She said.

I must admit that at this point a small smirk started to develop on my face. This woman did not give a crap about status or hierarchy. As we entered the room, she motioned for us to sit down in the two chairs next to her bed.

"How are you feeling today?" Jim began.

"How do you think? I'm dying," she said without skipping a beat. "But before you get all Jesus on me, I have a request to make of you."

"Of course," Jim said.

"Lean in," she said as she leaned toward us. Jim and I leaned in, but she said, "A little closer," so we both came in closer.

"Do not tell my children that I'm dying," she said as she looked us both square in the eyes. "They could not handle the situation. Do you understand?"

I was in shock. There I was standing there completely flabbergasted on my first day working for hospice. The children knew their mother was dying. The mother knew she was near death. There was a hospice chaplain in the house, and no one wanted to acknowledge the fact that there was an elephant in the room; a big, old grey elephant standing in the corner just shaking its head.

An hour later Jim and I were back in the car driving to the next house. Staring out the window, I began wondering what I had gotten myself into. Was I supposed to educate individuals about a service no one wants? One that no one wants to talk about or even acknowledge?

"Welcome to hospice," Jim said bluntly as he interrupted my thoughts.

The elephant in the room had now become my partner in crime. Over the next 17 years, we would help bridge the gaps between families and teach people how to talk openly about death and dying. My first day at hospice was just the beginning.

I had never seen the elephant in the room before. Maybe he was there all along, but I never noticed. In that same moment, I first realized how important communication was for connection and how connection to others is built on communication. It was the first lesson I learned on the first day at hospice, but it has taken me all 17 years to really embrace it and implement it to my life.

"Do not tell our mother that she is dying..."

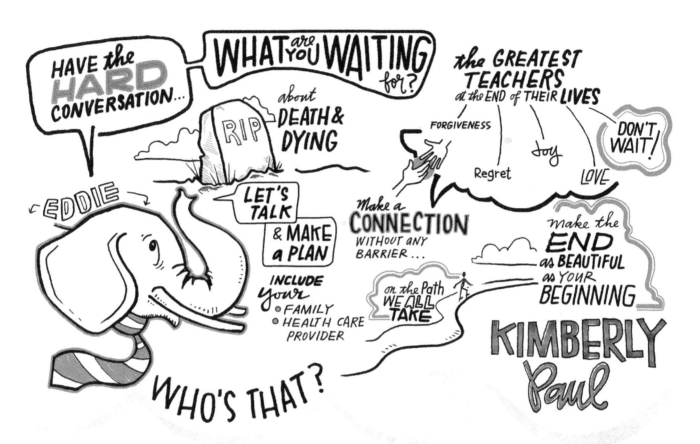

"Do not tell my children that I'm dying..."

"The tragedy of life is not death ...
but what we let die inside of us while we live."
—Norman Cousins

CHAPTER THREE

Life Lesson: It is the small stuff in the end that really does matter most.

"The simple things are also the most extraordinary things, and only the wise can see them." —Paulo Coelho

After working as the volunteer program manager for hospice for only eight months, I unexpectedly received a request from a social worker to find a German Shepherd for a family in the program. Completely shocked, I decided to get a few more details about the situation before I even began to search for a dog.

"Hey, Pam," I asked, "You really need a German Shepherd?"

"Yep," she replied with a smirk. "I'm working with a family in Hampstead that has requested a German Shepherd." I could see she was thinking there was no way I could find a dog to loan to this hospice patient.

"How am I supposed to find a dog for a family to keep for only a few weeks?"

"I don't know," she said, "but you seem to be a miracle worker with human volunteers. Maybe this will be an opportunity for you to stretch your boundaries."

Pam was a seasoned social worker with many years of experience, but clinical people could sense a creative person from miles away. I felt most of them wanted me to fail at the tasks they put before me and squash me like a bug under their rubber-soled shoes. I was inspired and determined to find someone to loan me a German Shepherd, but who would do something that insane?

"I'll need to meet the family prior to fulfilling this request," I said with authority. "I want to make sure I'm not going to put a dog in a dangerous situation."

"Sure, here is the address and the number," she said. "Good luck, rookie."

That same afternoon I found myself headed to Hampstead to meet the patient whose request was not for a volunteer, but for a dog. As I drove down the dirt road toward the modular home, I thought to myself that I must be the one who is insane.

As I walked toward the door, a sweet elderly lady welcomed me in before I could even ring the bell. "Come in," she said. "I'm Julie, Luke's wife. Please have a seat."

Without skipping a beat, she asked, "Do you think you could find a German Shepherd for us?" The look of hope in her eyes melted me.

"All I can do is try," I replied as I looked around the small but tidy house.

"Would you like to meet Luke?" she continued. "Lately, he mostly sleeps throughout the day."

I followed her down the hallway as she opened the door. "Luke, are you awake?" she asked. There was no answer. As we entered the room, I saw him lying there in his hospital bed looking at us with weak but open eyes.

As he reached out his hand I said, "Hi, Mr. Luke. I'm Kimberly. Someone told me you were looking for a German Shepherd to love on for a few days."

His eyes lit up. "I raised German Shepherds for many years," he said in a fragile voice, "and I would love to have one around the house."

"I can't promise anything, but I'll do my best."

After touching his hand, Julie led me back to the living room. "He has not gotten out of bed the last few weeks," she said. "I don't think he is doing well. I guess what I'm trying to say is that time is limited, so if you're unable to find us a dog we will understand."

"I'll do my best," I replied.

As I got into my Jeep, I was more determined than ever to find someone who would trust me and this family to take responsibility for a German Shepherd for two weeks. "This is going to be "easy-peasy," I said to myself with sarcasm.

When I got back to the office, I started calling shelters, friends, and breeders in the surrounding area looking for any options to fulfill Mr. Luke's wish. "Hello, I'm Kimberly," I began. "I work for hospice and was wondering if you would consider loaning one of your dogs to a hospice patient for a week or two."

"Excuse me?" one man replied at the other end of the phone.

"I know this is an unusual request," I said, "but I have a patient that is facing end of life who has raised German Shepherds all his life. He was wondering if you would consider allowing one of your dogs to stay with him for a few weeks."

"My mother had hospice," the voice responded.

"I hope it was a good experience," I said with my fingers crossed.

"I could not have gotten through that time without you guys," he said. "Why don't you come by on Saturday and let's talk about the arrangements."

"You would consider it, sir?" I asked.

"Let's just talk," he said with compassion. "I have a litter of puppies that are up for sale right now, but I also have a young female not yet in heat. She is a gentle girl, and her name is Duchess."

I set up the appointment for Saturday at 10 a.m. and I arrived a few minutes early at their home in the small town of Bolivia. Meeting me in the driveway, the couple led me to the backyard where I found 15 immaculate kennels housing the most beautiful Shepherds I had ever seen.

"Let me show you the babies first," he said as they all started barking.

I counted eight giant puppies following their mother's lead. They were both goliath and small at the same time. He opened the fence, and all came running at me. Some had colored ribbons marking they were sold, and others were eager for me to take them home.

Sitting on the ground drowning in puppy breath and kisses, one little girl fell asleep in my lap. She was obviously the runt of the litter, and as she slept, I fell in love.

"That pup likes you," the gentleman said.

"I wish I could keep her."

"You can have her for $800. I've knocked off a couple hundred 'cuz I like you."

"I wish I could, but I can barely make rent these days," I said.

"Are you new in these parts?" He asked.

"Yes. I recently moved from New York City, via Garner first, back to North Carolina," I said.

"You're a city gal, are you?" He said with a smile.

"Not really. I was raised in Virginia. I went to school at Meredith College in Raleigh. I was living in Garner for almost two years prior to moving to the coast."

"What brought you to the sea?" He said.

"A broken heart."

"Your folks still live in Virginia?"

"My dad does. He works for the Virginia State Police."

"Obviously you didn't get away with much growing up."

"Not really."

"Let's round these pups up and send them back to their mama."

I hated to part with that sleeping puppy, but I had two cats at home, and I knew a puppy would be too much for my roommate and me to handle.

"Follow me," he said. "I want to introduce you to Duchess."

Walking across the yard to the older dogs' kennels, we finally took the time to introduce ourselves. "She's the third one down," Mr. Jack said.

There I stood looking at the most beautiful dog I'd ever seen. Pacing in her kennel back and forth, she barked, "Hey daddy, open the door!"

Duchess had perfect German Shepherd markings. Her black and tan face was pristine. Her pointed ears were flawless. Her pink tongue was hanging out of her mouth in anticipation of the attention Mr. Jack was about to give.

As he opened the kennel, she whimpered at his feet. He looked down, patted her head and said, "Go see our new friend." She charged at me, all 70-pounds of her, with gentleness and love. She circled my legs and Mr. Jack simply commanded, "Sit down, Kimberly."

As I obeyed his order, Duchess started licking my face. "She's yours to take to your hospice patient if you want," he said.

"Are you serious?" I replied.

"Yes," he said, putting her back in her kennel. "Let's head inside and talk about the details."

As he rounded up Duchess, I thought, "Holy crap, I've actually done it!"

"Mr. Jack," I said, "Thank you so much, but I want you to understand that I cannot guarantee Duchess' safety. If that changes your mind, I will definitely understand."

"Kim, I'm a God-loving person and have been given a good life," he replied. "I want my dog back, but I know life happens and there is a chance something might happen to her. I was taught that if you're given much, much is expected. The dog is yours to take to the hospice patient until he dies."

"I don't know what to say," I said in awe of his candor.

"I do want to call the family to check on Duchess every day," he continued. "She might go into heat which could cut the trip short, but she is yours. You can pick her up on Monday morning. I'll supply the food and a leash."

"I'll provide you the patient and family information. I'm sure they would not mind you calling to check on Duchess."

Mr. Jack put out his hand, "Then it is a deal."

"Mr. Jack …" I started before I was interrupted.

"I know," is all he said.

I shook my head, climbed in my Jeep and realized that small miracles do happen every day. I picked up the phone to call the hospice family.

"I got a German Shepherd," I told Julie. "She'll arrive Monday morning."

"Luke's not doing well," she replied in a discouraged voice.

"Do you still want the dog?" I asked.

After a long pause she said, "Yes. It is what he wanted."

When I arrived Monday morning, Mr. Jack loaded dog food, a full page of instructions. and Duchess into my Jeep. Her leash was tightly attached to her collar.

"You're doing a great thing, Mr. Jack."

As I drove off, I realized there were several things that Mr. Jack and I didn't consider or discuss. Duchess had never traveled in a vehicle, she was not house-trained, and I had an hour drive ahead of me to deliver her to Mr. Luke.

I stopped by the main office at hospice to break up the trip. I was eager to show Pam, the social worker, that I had conquered her impossible task. I had successfully received a loan on a German Shepherd for her patient. I also wanted to walk Duchess around the office to meet some of the staff.

As we walked down the hallway, Duchess noticed her reflection in a mirror. She barked as if she had already been trained as a police dog raiding a drug house. There was no doubt the entire office staff knew there was a German Shepherd in the building.

Pulling Duchess away from the mirror, we proudly walked into Pam's office.

"I can't believe it," she said.

"Yep, a German Shepherd," I replied with a huge grin. "The breeder is allowing Mr. Luke to have the dog until … well … as long as he wants."

"How did you do this, rookie?"

"I have no idea," I said as we both bent down to love on Duchess.

Planning to drop the dog off at Mr. Luke's after the office pit stop, I asked Pam if she wanted to come along. "I need to reschedule a few appointments, but I would love to come," she replied.

When we arrived, Julie was standing at their door. "I didn't tell him about the dog just in case something happened," she said. As Duchess and I followed her down the hallway, Julie opened her husband's door and said, "Honey, we have a surprise for you." Mr. Luke looked weaker than the last time I saw him. It had only been five days since the request.

"Look honey …. a German Shepherd dog," Julie said.

I went to the other side of the bed, and as Mr. Luke leaned forward he could barely see Duchess. "See if she will jump on the bed," he said in a weak whisper.

I motioned for Duchess to jump on the bed. Before we knew it, she had jumped up, laid down, and was licking Mr. Luke's hand.

Asking Mr. Luke and Duchess to look in my direction, I took a photo. Pam stood in the doorway with tears in her eyes as Mr. Luke and Duchess stared into the camera.

"You guys are two of a kind," I said.

Mr. Jack had given me an entire truck load of dog food, Duchess' water bowl, and few of her toys from her kennel. As I unloaded the Jeep, Duchess walked through the house smelling everything as she became familiar with her temporary surroundings.

While Pam and I sat on the sofa sharing all the information Mr. Jack had provided for Julie, Mr. Luke suddenly appeared in the hallway. He did not say a word as he headed toward the kitchen to open a cabinet under the sink.

Astonished, I just looked at his wife. "He hasn't gotten out of bed in weeks," she said.

"DUCHESS"

I was amazed that a simple thing inspired action and lifted Mr. Luke's spirit. He was smiling. He was enjoying life, loving watching the German Shepherd pace around the house. It was such a simple thing that made a huge impact.

As we watched, Mr. Luke grabbed a box from under the sink and gingerly made his way to the sofa. He sat down, called Duchess over, and gave her a dog biscuit.

Leaving the house that day, Pam looked at me and said, "You did good, rookie."

"You too, old timer," I said with a smile.

Driving back to the office, I felt for the first time that I was where I was supposed to be. I realized that day that I didn't have to be in the hallways of a live television show or casting roles for a daytime drama in New York City to be important. I had found my home.

I'll never forget Mr. Luke's face when Duchess laid next to him in his hospice bed. Doing things for others, like finding that German Shepherd for him, gave me such deep satisfaction. I believe that day had an impact on a small corner of the world that was becoming my home.

****

Growing up, I had a German Shepherd named "RunJoe," that I adored. Whether good or bad, the breed was a very integral part of my childhood. When I was 11, a neighbor's German Shepherd bit me in the face. The owner told me not to bother the dog, but I was so sure he would like me that I put out my hand to pet him, and he jumped. It happened so fast.

With a tiny hole in my left eye and my lip bleeding profusely, my mother grasped the steering wheel with one hand as she slapped me with the other on the way to the hospital. After six stitches and an eye-patch, I was playing hopscotch the same afternoon.

Despite my scars, my love for German Shepherds remained. In 2011, I brought my beloved Haven into my world. She has been by my side for the last six years. After a former co-worker met Haven, she asked me, "Have you ever realized the resemblance between Haven and the dog in the bed with Mr. Luke?"

Maybe I got my Duchess after all.

"HAVEN"

"Life asked Death, 'Why do people love me, but hate you?'
Death responded, 'Because you are a beautiful lie
and I'm a painful truth.'" —Unknown

CHAPTER FOUR

Life Lesson: Death is universal and will touch us all.

"Death is a mighty, universal truth." —Charles Dickens

Working with individuals who choose to lean into their death has always amazed me. I realized they have a certain capability to see through all the crap that normal people get caught up in every day. They see more clearly and can break through the walls that have obscured their view from what matters most in life.

Those who embrace end of life find forgiveness mostly for themselves but also for others. They rekindle friendships and family connections. They allow anger to slip away and find solace in rare special moments. To do those things, they seem to find an authentic connection, or maybe even a universal impulse. As they strip down to their bare bones, they search for what is most important once they know life is limited.

I have learned that not all patients reach the "lean into" phase of dying. Some die as they have lived, but when someone at end of life breaks away from all the minutiae that comes with living, it is beautiful to see. They have an ability to lead you down a pathway that guides you to understanding the most important elements in life. I have been amazed by their stories. I have watched them interact and embrace living in the most authentic way I could ever imagine.

The first time I experienced such a transformation of individuals was on September 11, 2001. It was during the days and weeks that followed that I first began to understand the concept of the universal impulse.

What did the individuals on the planes and in those buildings teach us about human impulse on that fateful day? They were moments away from a horrifying, tragic, and unexpected death, yet they managed to find a cell phone and reach out to those they loved to say their goodbyes. We learned through the messages left behind that no life is certain. Our time on earth is fragile and can be taken away at any given moment.

Think about where you were on September 11, 2001. Did you feel the universal impulse as well?

On September 9, visiting a friend for the weekend, I found myself sitting in the hot sun watching the U.S. Open inside the Arthur Ashe Center, just eight miles outside of New York City. The stadium was in Queens and literally steps away from LaGuardia airport.

09-11-96

Poor as dirt, we somehow managed to snag two nickel seats to the tournament. Looking down on the court, the tennis pros were tiny specks swinging their rackets back and forth, grunting as the sun beat down on them and the crowd. From the top of the stadium, we could see the low flying planes coming in for landing. That was only two days before the world's view of low-flying planes would change forever.

Back in Wilmington, I recall sitting on the edge of my bed as I watched the "Today Show" and dressed for work. It was a beautiful Tuesday morning when suddenly Katie Couric reported that a small plane had flown into the World Trade Center.

I reached for the phone to call my cousin, Mel, who lived on the Upper West Side of Manhattan. "A plane has flown into the World Trade Center!" I said. While on the phone with him, another plane appeared on the TV screen. It was a passenger jet.

"How could two planes be that far off course?" I thought in my head.

"It's a terrorist attack," Mel calmly spoke into the receiver.

"I don't believe it," I said, but within moments the phone went dead.

Panicked, I called my cousin, Teresa, who was working for The Food Network in Manhattan. There was nothing but a busy signal. The phones were out of order, and all I could think about was my two closest family members in the midst of uncertainty. There was nothing I could do. I felt helpless, scared, and alone.

It would be years later before I finally learned the details about what happened after the phone went dead with Mel and what those relentless busy signals meant for Teresa and her family that unforgettable day.

Hearing how Teresa walked across the Brooklyn Bridge in desperate search of her two children was gut-wrenching. Knowing she found them and walked them back to their small apartment in Prospect Heights, just a few miles from ground zero, was inspiring.

This is Teresa's story firsthand.

****

It was an early Tuesday morning, and I was in a rush to get out the door. Working at The Food Network on the Upper West Side of Manhattan, I had to go in early to transcribe a few recipes for the upcoming "Emeril" show that would start filming later that week.

I opened the door to the kids' room. "Peter ... McKenna ... time to get up!" Stirring a 15-year-old and 11-year-old awake was never easy especially when leaving the house extra early.

Within 45 minutes, my car was loaded, and we were off to school. After drop-off, I headed toward Battery Tunnel. The traffic was much lighter than my regular 9:30 a.m. commute, and before I knew it, I was headed up the stairs to my office.

As I enjoyed the serenity of a quiet morning without co-workers, I began transcribing recipes and prepping for the next few days of filming. Needing to clarify a few things with my boss, I walked into her office to ask her a few questions.

I found her sitting in front of the television watching a morning news show reporting that a small plane had crashed into the World Trade Center. We were both concerned, but not worried. Trying to do business as usual, she answered my questions as we watched another plane crash into the North Tower.

It's a terrorist attack!" I screamed, grabbing my boss' hand. At that moment, all I could think about was my children.

The entire office immediately went on lock down for the next several hours. Uncertain about the possibility of even more planes crashing down to terrorize the city, no one could exit or enter our building.

When I realized the first tower had fallen, I knew I had to get to my kids. Gathering my thoughts, I walked to my office. My desk phone was ringing.

"Hi Mom." It was Peter. "The schools are on lockdown."

"Just stay there, I'll come for you and McKenna".

"They are trying to see if any parents can pick us up."

"I'll be there," I said with as much confidence as I could. I hung up the phone as the receiver shook in my hand.

Looking up, I found my boss standing in the doorway. "I can't stay," I said. "My ex-husband is in Italy. I am all they have."

"How are you going to get them?" she asked with tears rolling down her face. "The city is shut down. No one can enter or leave."

"I don't care if I have to swim across the East River. I'll get to them."

As we embraced, I grabbed my things and left the building. Leaving my car behind, I opened the door to the streets of New York City and found an eerie silence. There were no car horns blowing; nothing was normal. I started walking toward downtown … toward what is now known as ground zero.

The entire west side below Broadway was closed. I made my way over to the east side of the city. I remember looking up at the Empire State Building thinking it could be the next building to come down. The fear that consumed me gave me even more strength to get my kids home safe and sound.

The closer I got to the Brooklyn Bridge, I started seeing individuals covered with heavy ash. Some were bleeding. Other than asking people if they were okay, no one spoke.

I looked around and knew I was in the middle of a war zone. Everyone was in shock.

09-11-01

When I reached the bridge it had finally reopened, and the NYPD were allowing people to walk across. I took a moment to glance back and saw that the Twin Towers were no longer there. I knew in my heart that thousands of people had died. The smell of burning steel was so thick. It was the smell of death. I turned back toward the bridge on a mission to find my kids.

As I finally arrived safely at the school, the headmaster asked to see me. She sat down behind her desk and said, "Three of Peter's friends need a place to stay. One boy's parents cannot be located, another one's father is in the hospital and the other's home has been destroyed. Are you able to take them?"

I paused for a moment and wondered how I would feed all of us on a limited budget. "Of course," I said. So with three growing boys and my two children in tow, we all headed to my two bedroom Prospect Place apartment building.

I cooked two roasted chickens, mashed potatoes with parsnips, and green beans for dinner. After eating, we headed to the roof to witness firsthand what was being broadcast live on national television.

"We are together and safe tonight. That is all that matters," I said, grabbing my two kids' hands in mine.

Within two weeks, things started to feel a little normal. The kids were back in school, and I was back at work. Over the next six months, The Food Network provided chefs to cook meals for rescue workers on the Red Cross barge. We were instructed not to interact with them but only to cook and serve.

Those few months were surreal. I felt like I was sleepwalking through the destruction and was numb to the full impact of what had happened. One week I was back at work as if nothing had happened. The next week I was face to face with individuals tasked with recovering those buried underneath the rubble left behind by the worst terrorist attack on our soil since Pearl Harbor.

During my last week on the barge, I cut my finger prepping lunch. As I headed into the bathroom to rinse my wound, I found a young woman crying on the floor, just sitting there with her back against the wall.

"Are you okay?" I asked as I bent down toward her.

"I'll never be okay again," she muttered through her tears and anger.

I sat down next to her, put my arm around her and pulled her into me.

"There are so many body parts," she said sobbing. "How are we going to identify all of those people? How could someone have so much hatred for complete strangers?"

"I don't know," I said through my own tears, "but what I do know is that this city is grateful for all you are doing to search for their loved ones. You are the true heroes. I've never been so proud to call myself a New Yorker."

After a few minutes, I helped the young girl off the floor. She hugged me with a tight, unforgettable embrace. She was scared, and I was too. How would life ever be the same? For that brief moment, however, we were two strangers comforting each other in the women's bathroom on a barge in New York City's harbor. I realized the resolve and compassion human beings could have for others in the midst of tragedy.

In that instant, I felt grateful and lucky that my family was safe, but I also felt a deep rush of gratitude for complete strangers. As many fled the streets of New York City on that fateful day, there were many more who raced into the face of danger, hoping to save lives.

As the young lady exited the bathroom, I realized I didn't get her name. She made September 11th, 2001 as real to me as it would ever be in my mind. Even in her pain, she headed back out to identify another body, hoping to bring closure to one more family.

I turned toward the mirror and barely recognized myself. I realized then that if I had not gone into the city early that morning on 9-11, I would have been driving through the Battery Tunnel under the World Trade Center at exactly 9:30 a.m.

-Teresa

****

The events that unfolded on September 11, 2001, somehow changed all of us. We cut through the minutia and gave in to the universal impulse to reach out and connect with total strangers.

When I relate this human experience to the healthcare system we are currently living in, it horrifies me. One of the most important elements of that horrific day is that many people were able to reach out, say goodbye, and find and provide closure. I believe the existing state of our medical industry steals those fundamental needs away from dying patients by keeping the truth about their illness in the dark to keep false hope alive.

As individuals become aware that death is near, something universal tends to occur. The majority want to connect with those who mean the most to them. They want to find and provide closure. When healthcare professionals are not truthful with patients about their illness, they still put trust in their providers and believe they are not dying, despite what their weakening bodies are telling them and the overall decline in quality of life family members may witness.

When physicians do not speak the truth, they steal the last moments of a patient's life and prolong suffering. Family members and loved ones are cheated out of the chance to say their goodbyes. If one chooses to work with the dying, it is our duty to be factual, even if the prognosis is terminal. People should be given the full facts in order to make educated decisions moving forward about treatment or non-treatment. We as consumers must demand this from our healthcare system.

Relating back to that tragic day on September 2001, I think of those living in Manhattan and working at the Pentagon. I visualize the passengers on all four planes as they were coming down. Something universal did happen on 9-11. The simplicity of life became important again as its certainty was pulled out from under a nation.

People began to realize that life is not a guarantee. We witnessed neighbors helping neighbors. We saw fearless citizens join fire rescuers and police departments to save others in the midst of war. For the first time in a long time, our nation was united. We were all on the same side.

There is one self-evident thing I hold to be true in my heart. The dying … especially those who lean into their death … exemplify the importance of life. It has nothing to do with money, titles, or fame. Life and death are about connecting with those you love most and saying goodbye.

I don't think about those planes I saw flying over the Arthur Ashe Stadium just two days before 9-11 or the fallen World Trade Center anymore. I remember the life lessons I learned from those who died or came close to death on that terrible day so many years ago.

They taught me how to connect, how to say I love you, and how to say goodbye. Through the dying, I have learned to always tell my friends I love them and maintain my relationships with those who matter most.

"The events that unfolded on September 11, 2001, somehow changed all of us. We cut through the minutia and gave in to the universal impulse to reach out and connect with total strangers."

31

DRAGONFLY
Bar & Grill
Playa Tamarindo

"The fear of death follows from the fear of life.
A man who lives fully is prepared to die at any time."
—Mark Twain

CHAPTER FIVE

Life Lesson: Advocating for others will open your heart to truth.

*"Strong people stand up for themselves, but
the strongest people stand up for others."* —Unknown

It was a regular morning around the hospice office. Nurses were preparing for the day, social workers were making phone calls, CNAs were loading their cars with supplies, and admission nurses were rushing out the door to admit new patients. I was in my office, a closet really, that just happened to be across the hall from my executive director.

I was comfortable in my position as volunteer program manager. It had been two years since my first day at hospice. Having the best of both worlds, I was working closely with our hospice team. A hospice team consists of those working at the bedside of patients. In hospice we call them an interdisciplinary team, which includes a nurse, social worker, chaplain, a volunteer, and a physician. The team meets every two weeks to discuss the patient's care. My job was overseeing the volunteer piece of the team. Through my volunteers, I was meeting many new people in the Cape Fear region. I simply loved working with the volunteers.

I hung up the phone after assigning a volunteer to a patient in the Wrightsville Beach area. Looking up, I found my boss standing at my door.

"Hey, do you have a minute?" she asked.

"Sure."

I followed her into her office and sat down. The room was filled with photos of her children and grandchildren showcasing the vacations they had taken together over the years.

"What's up?" I asked.

"You're a social worker, right?" she asked with inquisitive eyes.

"Well, I have a bachelor's in social work ... so yes. But I've never really practiced being a social worker." I started to feel uneasy about the conversation. "Why do you ask?"

"We are really busy today, and two admission nurses have the flu. There is a family at the hospital that needs someone to talk to them about hospice care. Do you think you could do that?"

"All I would have to do is explain hospice care?" I replied.

"Yes," she said.

"Sure, I can go over there and talk to a few family members."

"Great. Janice will bring you the information. Are you sure you can do this?"

"Absolutely," I said confidently.

Within ten minutes Janice had delivered the information needed. I flipped through the paperwork: Eloise Smith, 87-year-old female. Diagnosis: Breast Cancer. Condition: Terminal. Refuses further treatment. Daughter is Jennifer Waters and youngest child. She is in shock and confused about next steps. 8th Floor, Room 205. I knew the 8th floor was the oncology wing of the hospital. I started to feel panic set in as I tried to gather my thoughts.

As I tried to maintain some confidence, I jumped into my Jeep Wrangler. It was only a short drive to the hospital, but for some reason I could not bring myself to start the vehicle. Several thoughts entered my head. Was I qualified to do this? I'm not a clinical person. I thought to myself that if I knew how to explain hospice services, I should be okay, right?

The thoughts continued. The best we could do for this daughter facing the end of her mother's life was send me? Overwhelmed by self-doubt and fear, I had to balance the playing field and examine in my head what I could offer this dying woman and her child. I could show up and just be present. I could provide compassion and empathy. I could listen. I decided that was going to be my plan.

I started my Jeep and drove toward the hospital. As I entered the lobby, I headed to the elevator. I pressed the number eight and started to sweat. As I exited the elevator the awareness of death was in the air. I knew most of these patients would never leave the hospital. You could see it in the face of each family member.

I walked toward the nurse's station and said, "Hi, I'm from hospice. I'm here to speak to Jennifer Waters."

The desk clerk stood up, looked around and pointed to a small waiting area to the left of the nurse's station. Without more instruction, she picked up the ringing phone, looked at me and nodded her head in the direction of Mrs. Waters. I took a huge gulp and starting walking toward her. I noticed she was leaning forward with her elbows on her knees. Her face was in her hands.

"Mrs. Waters?" I confirmed as I sat down across from her.

She was a woman in her mid-forties. She looked up at me with her swollen red eyes and said, "Yes, I'm Jennifer."

"I'm Kimberly from hospice."

Digging for a tissue in her purse, she simply said, "They told me you would be coming."

"Mrs. Waters, do you know what hosp ..." I stopped mid-sentence. I looked at this young lady struggling to find a tissue as she sat there broken-hearted and confused. "Mrs. Waters, are you okay?" I asked instead.

With tears filling her crystal blue eyes once again, she said, "I don't know. I'm scared."

I reached out to touch her arm, "I'm so sorry to hear your mother is sick."

"She's not getting any better," she said, as she wiped away more tears.

Still touching her arm, I asked, "What is the most important thing for you and your mother from this moment forward?

"I want to take my mother home," she said with hope in her eyes. "Can you help me get her home?"

"I think I can help you with that. Let me go speak to the desk clerk. I'll be right back."

As I walked away, I knew I had no idea if I could help her but knew I had to try. I approached the nurse's station. The desk clerk was on the phone solving issue after issue. After a few minutes, she hung up, looked at me and asked, "Can I help you?"

"Yeah, how do you get someone discharged from the hospital?"

"Are you referring to Mrs. Water's mother?" She asked.

"Yes," I said.

"Girl, she isn't going home."

"What do you mean? Isn't there a way to discharge Mrs. Smith and admit her to home hospice?"

"You're going to have to speak to God about that."

"God?" I asked.

"Yep, otherwise known as Dr. Dyer." She looked me up and down and with a smile, pointed me in the direction of Dr. Dyer. "Good luck child," she said with a smirk.

I walked over to the doctor as he worked on his charts.

"Dr. Dyer?" I asked.

"Yep," he grunted without even looking up.

"I'm Kimberly from hospice. I was asked to visit with Mrs. Waters and talk about hospice care for her mother."

"Yes?" he replied, still not looking up.

"Mrs. Waters would like her mother discharged with home hospice today if possible."

That got his attention. He stopped charting, looked up and down at me.

"Who are you?" he asked.

The way he said it made me feel uneducated and totally out of my scope of practice. It shook my nerves. "No one, just someone ... uh, I mean I'm from the local hospice trying to assist a family."

He looked at me for what felt like an eternity. He went back to charting and finally said, "She is too unstable to be transferred home. I'm really busy."

I started to walk away, but something made me turn around. "Excuse me, Dr. Dyer. I'm new..."

"I can tell," he barked.

"Yeah? Well I have a question for you."

"What is it?"

"Aren't all dying patients unstable?"

He put his chart down again and said, "I don't have time for this. She would never make it home."

"It is her dying wish to go home," I said with authority. "Her daughter wants to give this to her mother. If I can get the daughter to understand that her mother might die in transport, would you sign off on the discharge papers?"

"That is a lot of trouble for a patient who is actively dying," he said with even more authority. "Let's not even talk about the money involved to make this happen. My answer is no."

Taking a deep breath, I found myself confronting this doctor. "What if this was your mother, Dr. Dyer? Would you do it differently? If your mother wanted to go home to die among family instead of strangers coming in and out of your room at all hours of the night, would you do it differently? Mrs. Smith wants to die in her own bed among family without rules about visiting hours, with home cooked meals and ..."

"Wait!" he said sharply. Knowing I was about to be confronted in the worst possible way among a slew of clinical providers charting in the middle of the day, I cautiously looked up into Dr. Dyer's eyes. His face had suddenly softened.

"This is really that important to you?" he asked.

"No sir," I replied, pointing to the daughter wiping tears away in the small sitting area next to the nurse's station. "This is important to her. You can help her."

Dr. Dyer sat down in a desk chair, exhaled and said, "Okay. If the daughter is informed that there is a large possibility that her mother will die in transport, I'll sign the discharge papers."

"Great. That is all I can ask. Will you come with me to tell her?"

"Sure."

Dr. Dyer led the way toward Mrs. Waters. Sitting down across from her as I sat beside her, he began to say, "So ..." pausing as he tried to recall my name.

"Kimberly," I quietly said.

"So, Kimberly from hospice has informed me that you want your mother to be discharged today so she can receive home hospice care."

"My mother wants to go home," Mrs. Waters replied. "I want to do everything I can to get her back there.

"Is my mother dying?" she asked as she made eye contact with the doctor for the first time. As she clutched her hands together, I put my hand over hers.

Dr. Dyer looked her straight in the eye as he placed his hand on top of our hands and said, "Yes, your mother is dying."

Mrs. Waters looked down at the cluster of hands. Tears silently dropped from her cheeks.

"Are you okay if we try to get your mother home and she dies in transport?" Dr. Dyer asked.

"I think so."

"Can she be with her in the transport?" I asked.

"That is not protocol."

"I understand," I continued, "but we can break protocol for special circumstances, right?" I was desperate for Mrs. Waters to be with her mother throughout the entire process just in case her mother did pass on before she was able to get home.

"I'll see what I can do," Dr. Dyer said.

"Thank you so much," Mrs. Waters said as she reached out to shake his hand.

As Dr. Dyer and I walked back to the nurse's station to start the paperwork, he looked at me and said, "You sure are pushy."

"I know, I'm sorry. Her mother's last wish was to just go home."

"You're a good hospice nurse."

"Oh, I'm not a nurse," I said knowing that I was just a volunteer program manager using my degree in social work per my boss' request to help in a bind.

"You're not?" he asked, tilting his head at me.

"No, I oversee the volunteer department." The look on his face was priceless.

Within two hours, Mrs. Waters and I had packed up her mother's things and loaded them into her car. "If you want," I said, "I can drive your car to your mother's house so you can stay with her while she is being transported."

"Great," she replied. "We live only a few miles away."

As I shut the trunk, I watched Mrs. Waters head back into the hospital to be with her mother. She turned around and asked, "Oh, by the way, do you drive a stick?" I just grinned and nodded my head.

There I sat in someone else's car debating if I should start the engine once again. I could not bring myself to tell her it had been 10 years since my clutch driving days. I stalled four times and smelled the burning clutch the entire five miles I drove behind the transport vehicle.

When we arrived, the hospice nurse was waiting for us. As Mrs. Smith was lifted out of the transport, her smile was as large as life. I smiled as I watched Mrs. Waters escort her mother into the house she had lived in for fifty years.

"Can I have a hot chocolate now?" Mrs. Smith asked.

"Yes, mother, you can have a hot chocolate now."

Mrs. Smith lived for five more days in her small coastal cottage. Her children and other family members surrounded her as she left this world.

I felt honored to be a part of helping Mrs. Smith's daughter grant her mother's dying wish. I thought Dr. Dyer needed to know the outcome of signing the discharge papers that day. The morning after Mrs. Smith died, I ran by a local coffee house and grabbed two hot chocolates and headed to the 8th floor of the hospital.

When I arrived at the nurse's station, Dr. Dyer was charting again. "Excuse me, Dr. Dyer," I said.

"Oh no, not you again," he replied.

I smiled and handed him a hot chocolate. As we sipped together, I told him the story of Mrs. Smith's arrival home. I shared that she lived five additional days after coming home and left this world surrounded by love.

"Dr. Dyer," I said, "by signing the discharge papers that day, you changed three lives … Mrs. Smith's, her daughter's, and mine."

"I think there was four lives impacted that day," he replied.

"Really?"

As we looked at each other, sipping our hot chocolates in silence, I knew his life had been changed too. No more words needed to be said between us.

"See you around, Doctor D.," I said.

On the short drive back to the office, the voice of truth came to me. I realized that I never explained hospice care to Mrs. Waters and what our programs could do for her mother. That information wasn't important at the time. What was important was getting Mrs. Smith home. It took several departments at the hospital, our hospice team, and the transport team to logistically make it all happen. It took Mrs. Waters' willingness to fulfill her mother's last wish amid her own desperation at the thought of losing her mother.

Let's not forget about Dr. Dyer. He was the one who made the decision to help make Mrs. Smith's final wish come true.

Dr. Dyer and I would work together for the next 14 years, but that first meeting is one I'll never forget. We both learned a lot that day about a lot of things. We learned about our medical culture, about human spirit, about life, and death and about being human enough to do the right thing, even if it went against protocol.

You're my hero, Dr. D.

Still touching her arm, I asked, "What is the most important thing for you and your mother from this moment forward?"

"I don't forgive people because I'm weak.
I forgive them because I am strong enough to understand that
people are human and born to make mistake." —Marylin Monroe

CHAPTER SIX

Life Lesson: Forgiveness is the key to one's happiness.

"The only way out of the labyrinth of suffering is to forgive." — John Green

Throughout life you cross paths with individuals whose stories tend to radically change your entire point of view on certain things. I was profoundly changed by my encounter with a man, I'll call him Mr. Frank, on what seemed to be a typical day at hospice.

I mentioned Mr. Frank's story during my 2015 TEDx talk, but it is only now that I share the full story behind the man who asked me, "What are you waiting for?" I often think about Mr. Frank and Ms. Linda and reflect on the courage it took for Ms. Linda to forgive.

Their story is not just a lesson on how to forgive, but also one that teaches how to accept forgiveness. It is one of the most valuable lessons I have learned throughout my years working with hospice patients. I'll never forget Mr. Frank's story, and Ms. Linda who reminds me to believe in second chances. Here's their full story...

****

I had recently started to assist the marketing department to help expand awareness of hospice services outside the volunteer program I managed. My personal goal was to focus on the patients and their families' stories instead on what our agency could do for them.

I somehow found a way for them to share their personal experiences with hospice care to further our outreach efforts.

It is hard to find individuals who want to share their stories when coming to terms with end of life. With the help of our social workers, however, we were obtaining enough interviews to showcase at least one personal story per month.

At the time, the Festival of Trees was our biggest fundraiser of the year. Held in downtown Wilmington, the festival was a community event sponsored by local businesses who purchased trees and decorated them to raise funds for hospice.

The only problem was, despite how beautifully decorated the trees were, they still did not tell the personal stories of our hospice families. I wanted to share our patients' experiences to educate our community on how their donations were going to be allocated. I also wanted to take pictures of our patients and families and place the photos in a collage to create an exhibit of the images. As our team gathered photographs and personal accounts throughout the year, our hopes were to calm our community members' fears about death and dying and hospice services in general.

This project was one of my favorites. It was also one of the hardest to implement. Taking individual photographs and writing families' stories led to an intimate connection with all the faces displayed on those huge oversized displayed boards. The result bridged the gap between our community and the patients allowing all to see hospice patients as living persons worthy of celebrating their lives.

With each story we collected, we would cry, laugh, then cry again through the process. Each person became part of my own personal life story. Most of the time, when the trees arrived between Thanksgiving and Christmas, the patients who were highlighted had already passed away. The family members, though, loved walking through the winter wonderland of trees and found solace and comfort in seeing a lasting tribute to their loved ones.

The photographs captured rare moments for those left behind. I spent weeks after each festival visiting families and providing them with the pictures and stories to cherish forever. These meetings were extensive and emotional, usually lasting close to an hour over coffee. I connected with many families over the years who still occasionally send me articles and notes to my home address. You never realize the impact you have on others when you walk beside them during the final days of losing a loved one.

Late in November 2003, I was running around trying to finalize the photographic journey for that year's festival. Only weeks away, I needed one more patient interview to finalize the project. As I worried about time, a nurse from our hospice care center called.

"I have someone that would like to share their story," she said with excitement. "When can you come?"

"I'm swamped during the day, but I can come by after dinner tonight if that works," I said with a sigh of relief.

"Hold on, let me ask."

I waited for a few minutes, "Yep. That will work."

"Awesome," I said. "Thank you so much."

It had been a long day, but I managed to arrive at the hospice care center a little before 7 p.m. It was a Wednesday evening with a crisp, cool breeze that reminded me winter was coming yet still warm enough to enjoy an open window. As I arrived at room seven, there sat a lady in her fifties outside open double doors in a room that overlooked a small garden; she was holding Frank's hand.

"Mr. Frank?" I asked.

The lady stood up, kissed his forehead and started to gather her things.

"Yes, that is me," he replied. "Are you the one that wants to hear my story?"

"That's me," I replied.

As Frank walked to his bed, I could tell he was weak but had a certain inner strength about him.

"Don't forget to wash my favorite sweater, Linda."

"I'll remember," she said.

After she gathered a few more items, Linda said her goodbyes and exited the room.

"Is Linda your daughter?" I asked.

"Something like that."

As he settled into his bed, Frank asked me to shut the doors to the garden, pull up a chair and without much pause started talking.

"I'm a fortunate man," he began. "I've had a long life. I'm so happy to be surrounded by such good people."

"Sounds like a good life."

"Please don't misunderstand me," he continued. "You are young and have your entire life ahead of you. Be prepared to make a few mistakes. As much as I feel fortunate in my life, I feel huge regrets, too." He paused for a long moment. Feeling young and uncertain, I was uncomfortable by the silence.

"We all have regrets," I said.

He grabbed my arm, pulled me forward and asked, "What are you waiting for? Fix it. When you are young, you don't realize how fast time passes by. "You're too young to have big regrets …" he said, releasing my arm. "At least not like mine. You're kind, but I know by looking at you, you never murdered anyone."

"What?" I thought I had misunderstood what he just said.

"I was young and dumb. I was foolish," he began to explain. "I lived in the inner city and got involved with people I shouldn't have. I was 16-years old when I started stealing and robbing houses. I sold drugs. I was in a gang. It was the way of life."

"I could make excuses, but I won't," he continued. "Everything I did, it was my choice. I was 18 and for the very first time, I was given a gun. We were watching this house for about a week. They weren't supposed to be there, but they were. I went in through the back door, headed toward the living room when this lady ran toward me with a baseball bat. I didn't think. I shot her before I even knew what I was doing. She was bleeding and not moving when I noticed a young child standing in the doorway. I didn't know what to do. I ran," he said, as tears filled his eyes. "I ran. Can you believe that?"

I felt his pain linger in the room with every word he spoke. Still a little nervous, I could not help but reach out and touch his hand, but no words came out of my mouth. I was in shock at how this lovely man could have ever been that stupid kid. I just shook my head slowly back and forth.

"Believe it," he said, "The police found me less than 24 hours later. It was a relief. The first thing I asked the police was about that young girl. They would not tell me anything. You can't blame them. I was a thug. I didn't know I killed the woman until I went to court. I was being accused of 2nd degree murder. The trial lasted three days and I was sentenced to life in prison."

As he paused, I just looked at him. I can't tell you what was running through my mind at the time. I do recall looking to see if he was handcuffed to the bed, but he wasn't. I thought maybe I should end the conversation and slowly back out of the room, but I didn't. My hand was still on his, and he gently squeezed it. The gesture brought me back to the present and our eyes met.

"Are you scared of me?" he asked.

You know what they say—fake it until you make it. Well, I faked it.

"No," I said, pulling my hand away.

"I'm not that person any more. I was saved."

Thinking he found salvation in God or Jesus or some other higher power, I listened as he continued to explain.

"I was saved by the power of forgiveness. I spent 53 years behind those prison walls. The first decade or two I was angry, but I started to feel safe within the walls of that prison."

"In all those years," he said, "I had only one visitor. It was around my 60th birthday when a guard came to my cell and told me someone was there to see me. My curiosity got the best of me; I had to see who knew me or who actually wanted to know me. I sat in this closed off, small room for at least an hour. When the door opened, a guard escorted a young woman toward me. I stood up, but I didn't recognize her."

"She sat down across from me," he said. "She was crying."

He took me back to their conversation.

"I'm here to ask for your forgiveness," the stranger said.

"Do I know you?" Mr. Frank asked.

"You killed my mother," she bluntly stated. "I'm here to ask you for your forgiveness."

I was in complete shock once again. Could this woman be that child in the doorway from so many years ago?

"I killed a woman and left her dying in front of a young child," he said to his visitor.

"I was that child," she replied.

"What have you done that needs my forgiveness? I should be begging you ..."

"I need you to forgive me for the hatred I have for you," she interrupted. "If you can do that, I want to try to forgive you for taking my mother's life."

"You have every right to hate me," Mr. Frank told her.

"My hate can't hurt you," she replied. "It has only hurt me for the past 40 years. It is time to let go and move forward."

"She asked me to pray with her," Mr. Frank said to me. "She reached out and took my hand. While she was praying, something happened to my heart. I began to cry—cry hard. Here was the child that I left alone while her mother lay dying in front of her and she was holding my hand and praying for me. I kept saying over and over…'I'm sorry, I'm so sorry.' "She stood up and walked over to me," he continued. "I stood up. She embraced me. I couldn't remember the last time someone hugged me that tight. As she hugged me, she whispered in my ear, 'I forgive you and now it is time for you to forgive yourself."

"I put my arms around her, hugged her back, and thanked her," he told me.

Mr. Frank said, "She gave me a Bible that day. She highlighted a passage … Jeremiah 29:11. "For I know the plans I have for you, says the Lord, plans for good intentions, to give you a future with hope."

"When she left that day, I thought I would never see her again," he said.

"She came back to see you?" I asked surprised. I thought forgiveness was one thing, but to create a relationship and maintain it was beyond anything I could imagine.

"Yes. Every month," he replied. "She had become a lawyer. That little girl was now a lawyer in the big city. Every month for ten years she came to visit me. I remember one day she came in so excited."

"I think I finally found it!" she exclaimed.

"Found what?" Mr, Frank asked her.

"I found a technicality from your trial that might have been overlooked," she responded.

"You were interviewed by the police without a lawyer present after you requested representation. It is documented in the records."

"What does that mean?" Mr. Frank asked her.

"You asked for representation and were denied. I think I can get you out of prison," she said.

49

"I spent the last 50 years in this prison. I grew up here. There is no life for me on the outside," he told her.

"You were a stupid kid that grew up on the wrong side of the tracks," she said. "You deserve a chance to live outside these walls."

"I don't have anyone. I don't know where my family is, or if they would even want me back in their lives," Mr. Frank told her.

"You have me and my family. Let me help you," she selflessly offered.

"It took Linda eight years and appeal after appeal," Frank said as he turned to meet me eye to eye. "I was 76-years old when I walked out of prison three days before Christmas in 1993."

"Where did you go?" I asked.

"I went home with Linda," he replied. "She was married, and her husband was also a lawyer. She had two grown children with their own families scattered throughout the state. She took my hand and told me she had a small guesthouse. Linda took care of me. I would work odd jobs, but she helped me get a small settlement from the state."

"Do you live in Wilmington now?" I asked.

"No," he said. "Linda and her family come to the beach every other December to celebrate the holidays. I was in hospice care up north due to this old heart of mine. It doesn't want to work anymore. They said I could transfer to this hospice so I could be closer to my family."

"Linda?" I asked.

"The only family I have," he replied.

I looked up at the clock. It was 10 p.m. Three hours had flown by, and Mr. Frank looked tired.

"Can I get you anything?" I asked.

"No, I'm just an old, tired man that needs some sleep," he softly said.

"Mr. Frank, I haven't taken any pictures, and I need you to sign a release form. Do you want me to come back another day, so you can sleep?"

"That will be great," he said.

I gathered my things, walked over to the bed and touched Mr. Frank's hand. "Why do you think she forgave you?" I asked.

"She didn't do it for me," he said. "She did it for herself. All the other things that came after that day she forgave me for was for her mother. She wanted me to have a chance at a life her mother never had, and she wanted me to feel loved."

I looked at Mr. Frank for a long time. I did not see the stupid kid that made those horrible mistakes over 60 years ago. All I saw was a kind and gentle man who was well-loved.

"I'll see you soon," I told him.

"Okay," he said.

I walked out of Mr. Frank's room wondering if I could have done what Linda did so many years ago. Could I forgive someone for hurting someone I love … for killing someone I love? I don't know if I could find the courage to forgive and then welcome them into my life. It was the ultimate forgiveness. I could not grasp the road Linda chose to take, but we all should be who we are called to be … humans and forgivers.

On the way home that night, I kept thinking of Mr. Frank and his story. Is there a reason for everything that happens in life? I'm not sure, but what I did understand was that somehow Linda's life was richer because she welcomed Mr. Frank into it. As I closed my eyes that evening, still in awe from all I had heard, I wondered if I had someone that needed my forgiveness.

It was Friday morning before I could get back to the hospice care center. When I arrived at room seven, Mr. Frank was no longer there. The room had been cleaned and prepped awaiting the next hospice patient.

Racing to the nurse's station, I asked, "Where is Mr. Frank?"

"He died last night," one of the nurses replied.

Bewildered, I just stood there with my camera around my neck as the unsigned release form slipped from my hand onto the floor. I had no words.

"Don't worry, Kimberly," the nurse said. "His lovely family was with him."

I tried several times to get in touch with Linda and the family but never received a return phone call. Mr. Frank was never included in the Festival of Trees. It just wasn't meant to be.

As I walked through the festival that year, the lights of hope shined a little brighter and the songs of joy rang out even louder. I found my own way to recognize a man known to me as Mr. Frank and a lady who forgave and loved him. As I squeezed behind the 25-foot display of photos and stories collected, I carefully maneuvered myself through the extension cords. I reached into my backpack and pulled out a piece of paper that read: "To Mr. Frank and Ms. Linda, thank you for teaching me about forgiveness on the eve of this holiday season, 2003."

"I looked at Mr. Frank for a long time. I did not see the stupid kid that made those horrible mistakes over 60 years ago. All I saw was a kind and gentle man who was well-loved."

"You know that place between sleep and awake;
that place where you can still remember dreaming?
That's where I will always love you.
That's where I will be waiting."
—Peter Pan

CHAPTER SEVEN

Life Lesson: Unconditional love can change the world.

"Even after all this time the sun never says to the earth you owe me.

Look what happens with a love like that. It lights the whole sky." —Hafiz

Everyone has a story about how they end up where they are. Circumstance, happenstance, and a very special person transformed my life almost 20 years ago and ignited a passion that I'm now living.

After leaving New York City, I moved back to a small town outside of Raleigh, N.C., known as Garner. I fell in love for the very first time with a boy that happened to be a Garner police officer. His dream was to one day become an FBI agent.

I refer to him as "Apple," for many reasons.

Our relationship was full of respect, love, laughter, and adventure. Apple opened new doors to different ways of thinking. He exposed me to movies such as "Down the Rabbit Hole" and several books by Stephen Hawking. Apple rarely watched television and read all the time.

He loved good food, cooking, and rock climbing. He changed me in so many ways.

When Apple was accepted to the FBI Academy, he chose to dedicate his time to becoming the agent he dreamed of as a child. We mutually agreed to briefly halt our relationship, making promises to reconnect after his graduation. I had professional aspirations of my own, so it made perfect sense.

Our last weekend together was magical. I remember clearly driving away in my Jeep Wrangler heading east and watching his Del Sol disappear in my rearview mirror as Apple drove north. I felt overwhelmed and grateful at the same time. I was so thankful for the emotions I could feel toward another human being. I was not afraid, because I knew in time we would be together again.

That was the last time I saw him. There were no cards, phone calls, or emails after that last magical weekend. What I thought was a pause in our relationship, allowing both of us time to obtain our individual goals, was actually a break-up. I was devastated.

I was haunted by the small town of Garner after he left. Memories of our relationship replayed in my mind every time I passed a restaurant or movie theater. The questions lingered. Nothing at all—not even a phone call or email.

In search of a major change to jump start my life again, I packed my things and moved to the eastern coast of North Carolina in 1999. I chose the coastal town of Wilmington hoping to work once again in the film industry.

Wilmington's film and studio opportunities were on hiatus when I arrived, so I took a position with a hospice organization overseeing their volunteer program. It was a temporary position—or so I thought.

My life seemed to be gaining traction. I was working full time, living at the beach and meeting new people. It had been five years since my relationship with Apple had ended. A co-worker with hospice asked me to be a bridesmaid in her wedding, and I reluctantly accepted. At the age of 34, I was not interested in purchasing a dress I would never wear again. I was also not interested in being portrayed as the mid-thirties spinster in the wedding party who had not found her soul mate, but out of love for the bride I did it anyway.

The night before the wedding, I arrived late to the rehearsal dinner. Overlooking the Atlantic Ocean, The Oceanic restaurant at Wrightsville Beach can be magical. Running in, I picked a random table and struck up a conversation with a lovely group attending the dinner. They were strangers to me.

Making small talk, a lady next to me mentioned her husband used to work for the police department in Garner, N.C. Without much pause, I said, "I used to know someone that worked for the Garner police department."

"Who?" she asked.

"Apple," I responded as casually as I could.

"Wow," she said as she continued to eat. "Now that's a sad story."

My mind began to race. Was he killed in the line of duty? I chose to not say a word and let her share her next thought.

"He died," she said.

"He was in love with this girl in Garner," she continued, "and broke up with her and never told her that he had cancer. He died in hospice care only 18 months later."

I was completely paralyzed. I don't recall much after that moment, but I do know I managed to reach out and grab that woman's arm.

I looked her straight in the eyes and said, "You're talking to the girl."

****

The summer of 2000 found me working with hospice off Wellington Drive in Wilmington. Knowing Apple had graduated from the FBI academy over a year ago and was relocating to Salt Lake City, I was trying to move on with my life. And although I was dating again, something was still missing. I needed to find closure and come to terms with the end of our relationship.

Before the days of Google, I sat at my desk, picked up the phone and dialed 411 for Salt Lake City's information line. I asked for Apple's number, and it was given to me.

Hesitating just a moment, I picked up the phone and called.

"You've reached the Apple's resident, we are not home right now," a woman's voice said over the answering machine. "Please leave a message."

I hung up.

It would be years later before I found out the truth about Apple. Instead of him getting married and moving on with his life as I had assumed, he had died just two months prior to me making that call. I had even unknowingly dialed the wrong number.

Although my assumptions were wrong, the call did help me find some sense of false closure to move forward in life ... until that fateful night in April when I was late for a rehearsal dinner.

****

I looked her straight in the eyes and said, "You're talking to the girl —"

The following day I had to be a bridesmaid in a church packed with happy people celebrating my co-worker's marriage. Me? I could barely stand. Still in shock, I wanted to be anywhere but there.

I felt my entire world crashing down around me. I wanted to scream at the top of my lungs and make the world stop moving until my questions were answered. As I stood there watching two individuals exchange their wedding vows, I knew what I had to do for myself. I had to find out what happened to Apple. I had to ask, "Why?"

Apple's family lived in Indiana. Other than talking with them over the phone, I had never met them. I was determined, though, to find them and ask the questions that now haunted my every moment, my every movement.

The following Monday morning, sitting at my hospice desk now as Vice President of Communications and Outreach, I started my Google search. The last name Apple and the state of Indiana were all I had to go on. The search returned over 200 hundred Apple names with phone numbers. This was going to be a long process. Remembering they lived in a small town, I randomly picked one.

I picked up the phone several times, but could not pull myself together enough to press the numbers. What if I found out he didn't love me? Maybe the woman at the rehearsal dinner had been overly dramatic. Why didn't he tell me he was sick?

Then I realized it had been almost seven years since he drove away from me in Garner. No matter the answers, no matter the outcome, my heart was already broken. I just needed to know.

I picked up the phone and pressed the buttons. A woman answered.

"Hello", she said.

"Yes, I'm looking for Apple's parents," I said nervously. "He was a Garner police officer and continued into the FBI.

"You're speaking to his mother," she said.

"What?" I asked.

"I'm Apple's mother," she said.

"My name is Kimberly Paul. I knew your son," I told her.

"I know who you are." Her voice turned to sadness.

"You do?" I asked surprised.

"Of course. You're the girl my son loved," she said.

"What happened?" I asked with such confusion. The conversation continued for another hour.

"Will you come visit us?" Apple's mother asked. "The family would really like to meet you and get to know you. We try to get together on Apple's death date to celebrate his life. Would you consider coming out to celebrate with us?"

"I would love to." I replied.

I arrived in Indiana only five weeks later. Apple's mother picked me up from the airport. We drove back to her house and immediately started talking, sharing stories and pictures.

"Why didn't he tell me he was dying?" I asked with tears in my eyes. There was a long pause.

"He often spoke of the time you guys were dating," she began. "You had lost someone from high school to cancer and it hit you hard. Do you remember what you used to say to him when he worked the night shift as a police officer in Garner?"

With tears rolling down my face, I replied, "Yes. I told him to be safe. I told him I respected that he loved being a police officer, but I couldn't bear to lose another person."

"He heard you," she said.

I could not believe what I was hearing. I gasped, put my hands to my mouth and started to sob. Apple's mother stood up, walked over to me, wrapped her arms around me, and held me for what seemed like hours.

"I need to show you a few things prior to the rest of the family coming home," she said pulling from our embrace.

Apple's mother led me into her bedroom. On top of the chest of drawers was a picture of me and Apple. She picked up the framed picture and said, "I look at it every day."

"There is one more thing," she said. She led me to the garage door and opened it. There was the Del Sol, the car he had when we dated, the car that drove him north the day I last saw him. His family had kept it.

"Can I sit in it?" I asked.

"Of course," she replied.

I sat in that Del Sol for over 20 minutes. It still smelled of him. I shut my eyes, and within moments I could see Apple, smiling, driving us through downtown Raleigh. With the wind blowing through the windows, NPR on the radio, we were on our way to see an off-beat movie and then pizza in the Five Points district.

I didn't want to open my eyes, but a knock on the window brought me back to reality. This was my life, not a book or a movie, but my life. I felt this overwhelming responsibility that my life was not just mine anymore. I would have to head back to Wilmington and explain my broken heart to friends that had never heard of a boy I called Apple.

"Are you okay, dear?" Apple's mother asked.

As I climbed out of the car I said, "I will be. I think. I think I will be."

It took several years to come to terms with the finality of losing Apple. Time helped fill in the details of Apple's final months, and I got the answers I was looking for.

For so many years prior to knowing the truth, I wondered what happened. I knew he wouldn't leave me without an explanation, but my own self-doubt convinced me that he just didn't love me. It just wasn't meant to be. Only on that day, back in April, at that randomly selected table at a rehearsal dinner, the one I didn't want to go to, did the truth finally find me. I guess I was ready to hear that truth and come face to face with the reality that Apple, my Apple, died at the age of 30 from melanoma.

So, there once was a boy I loved. He became an FBI agent. He broke my heart but saved my life. It was 18 months, almost to the day, after he left me that he died in hospice care in Indiana.

I often wonder what would have happened if he had told me the truth about his illness, but I stop myself and embrace the unconditional gift he gave me. My head says, "I could have done this, or I could have been by his side." But my heart, well, I'm not so sure I would have recovered from such a great loss at such a young age. It happened exactly how it was supposed to happen. It happened how he wanted it to happen.

Some might romanticize this story, but I assure you reality doesn't need anything but the truth. Apple and I shared a deep connection. It was magical how everything conspired to come together to reveal the truth to me on that fateful day in April.

I'm grateful I knew Apple. I'm grateful that I loved Apple. He changed me in ways I could have never imagined. I'm grateful I now know the truth.

My leg now adorns an apple that resembles a heart on my left inside ankle. It is shielded from the outside world, but it is a permanent reminder of and tribute to the connection I shared with a guy I called "Apple."

So, the Apple Effect is when you love someone enough to let them go; you prefer to break their heart to save them from unbearable suffering. In essence, you save their life.

And that is exactly what Apple did for me. He saved me in every way a human being could save another. For that, I will be forever grateful.

I feel Apple next to me every day., walking with me, and teaching me to live boldly and fully embrace life and death on my own terms.

"APPLE"

"Enjoy the little things in life, for one day you will look back and realize they were the big things."
—Unknown

CHAPTER EIGHT

Life Lesson: Always ask for what you want ... because you just might get it.

"Ask for what you want and be prepared to get it." — *Maya Angelou*

It was hard to return to hospice after learning about Apple's death. I didn't know grief could be so heavy. Suddenly, hospice became very personal to me. Every patient somehow reminded me of Apple. I knew I was grieving, but I had a hard time fully understanding the happenstance of the recent events in my life. It was hard to explain to others. So, I found solace in the children's art room with huge beanbags when the days at hospice seemed to be too much for me. I could melt into the overwhelming softness that wrapped around me like a warm hug as my eyes raced over children's artwork working through their own grief. It was sort of fitting, because Apple always loved children.

Surrounded by the comforting hug of the beanbag, I often thought about the questions I never asked Apple. The questions that will never have answers. As I reflected, I questioned my own actions. What was I so afraid of? It would be a heaviness that I had to learn to carry with me, a lesson in life to be more vulnerable. It is a lesson I still struggle with to this day.

****

For those working in palliative care, end of life can get heavy at times, especially when a co-worker is facing their own serious illness. Many times, I found myself engulfed in that giant beanbag in the children's art room on the first floor of the hospice administrative building. I would shut the door, cry, meditate and even pray for the heaviness to be lifted. I would also search for the strength to assist other fellow staff grieving the loss of a co-worker as we continued to do business as usual.

I wish I could tell you my visits to the beanbag were few, but it would not be the truth. I remember sitting on the beanbag staring at a green balloon attached to a bridge in the memorial garden, placed in honor of our co-worker, Tracy. She was a young Irish mother with bronze-like red hair who had a personality that matched the fiery glow. She divorced a few years earlier, found love again, and was raising two strong boys when a serious illness crossed her path. She opted to treat her illness aggressively, hoping to see her boys grow up and become men.

Over the next few years, Tracy would feel better and come back to work. Then somehow the disease or the treatment would put her back in bed again.

There were a few things that stood out to me during this time. I noticed that our hospice organization wasn't as good at treating seriously ill employees with the same unconditional support that we offered our patients. We had become a thriving business, Tracy's position was still open, and work needed to be done. It was a very difficult situation.

On the other hand, the fact that Tracy was only two years older than me hit me hard. She arrived at our hospice care facility as a patient only days prior to her death. I don't recall how long she lived with her illness, but I know it was only a few years.

So, there I sat on the beanbag once again trying to cope with a co-worker's death. As I stared at the green balloon dancing in the wind, I began to ponder the question, "Have I impacted someone's life enough to be remembered so quietly, but so impactfully?"

What makes this life so precious? I sometimes wonder if it is because death is final. Life has two bookends. We all know that one day we will die, but we avoid the reality. I wonder why.

Then there was Anne, a 56-year-old co-worker facing a serious illness that sent me to the beanbag once again. She was an employee that I managed, a co-worker that made you want to live and celebrate everything. A co-worker that lived through Katrina. A person whose heart never left New Orleans. A person working at hospice, facing her own serious illness in the prime of her life.

It wasn't fair. It wasn't supposed to happen. Within a year, Anne decided that treatment was no longer an option. She leaned into her dying days with such celebration. Her last night at home was spent with her sisters eating a happy meal from a local fast food resturant, laughing and loving. Two days later she left this world behind. The roommate she knew as cancer was too annoying to live with, so she moved out and started a new adventure.

On the day we lost Anne, I wanted to find peace in the beanbag once again, but as I walked into the art room, I found our healing arts coordinator working with a hospice patient on a painting. Ironically, he was instructing her on artistic technique, almost giving her tips on how to be a better artist. With a straight face, Lorraine took the advice and thanked him just as I walked through the doorway.

"Hey Kimberly," she said. "Come in and meet the artist."

The 83-year-old hospice patient said to me, "Wow, you're what we would call a looker back in New York City in the 30s!" I chuckled, and so did Lorraine.

I do believe flattery gets you everywhere. I melted within moments of the introduction.

"What are you working on?" I asked, looking at his work.

"Well, beautiful, this is what we call a watercolor," he responded, still sweet-talking me. It was a stunning floral.

"When I'm done, this one is for you," he said. "I can't buy you flowers, but I can paint them."

"You're a mess," I teased back.

"I'm glad you noticed," he said with a wink.

On the day my heart ached because of the loss of another co-worker, I found solace and warmth ... not in the comfort of the beanbag, but in the comfort of the eyes of a dying artist in hospice care.

"I better get back to work, Casanova," I said.

"I'm here every Tuesday. Stop by again," he said.

So, over the next four weeks, I would visit with the artist on Tuesday. I learned about his life as Lorraine snickered under her breath at his unwavering flirtations with me.

"You should come over and let me cook you my favorite meal of all time," he suggestively proposed.

Lorraine eyeballed the situation, obviously wondering how I was going to get myself out of this one.

"Sure," I said. "As long as your art teacher can come too."

The night at his house was one of effortless joy. As Lorraine and I watched the hospice patient cook dinner for us and his family, the evening became full of simple pleasures and tenderness. I knew this patient was dying, and although he was breathless at times over the hot stove, he refused assistance and simply enjoyed serving his family and two new friends one last time.

His two sons were present and had totally inherited their father's flirtatious personality. It was overwhelming to be shown so much attention as they knew their father was dying, but I didn't care. I watched this hospice patient, this man, knowing death was near wanting just one thing: to cook, be with his family, and enjoy good conversation around his dinner table.

The conversation came so easily that night. It was as if I was an extended family member catching up on lost times, not a paid employee at hospice. I lived his life vicariously through the stories he shared. I found myself changing as I watched this dying man. I was seeing life from a different perspective. I found myself becoming more aware of the small things in life. It made me think this entire dying thing was given a bad reputation, because this man was living ... not dying.

The last Tuesday I saw him we had a great visit. As I started to leave and head back to my office, something unexpectedly happened. I was educated on the importance of a goodbye.

"You know when we depart in New York, we usually kiss one another," he announced without his eyes leaving the easel.

"Really?" I asked.

"Yep," he said.

As I bent down and kissed him on the cheek, he said, "That is not how we kiss goodbye in New York."

He turned toward me, looked me in the face, closed his eyes and puckered his lips. I looked at Lorraine. She provided no support whatsoever and leaned back in her chair to watch what was about to unfold.

What do you do when a dying man asks for a kiss on the lips? Well … you do it.

I bent down and I kissed him while his eyes were still closed. On the lips. As I stood back up, I noticed my boss in the doorway watching.

As I walked past her she said, "You'll do anything for a hospice patient."

"It was his dying wish," was all that I could muster up to say.

A few days later Lorraine stood at my office door with the floral watercolor in hand. There were no words needed. I knew the artist had left this world, and the painting was his final gift to me. He made me laugh, he made me blush, and he made me feel important.

Isn't that what we hope we do for others throughout this journey called life? I hope one day, if I'm ever a hospice patient, that I'm painting or writing when some young, attentive person crosses my path and pauses to learn something about me and my life. I hope I have the same guts to be so bold to ask for a kiss.

I embraced Lorraine as tears ran down our faces. We were in complete awe that we knew this man, an artist, prior to his death.

****

In the Fall 2016, I ran into Sherry Parker, a long-time friend and co-worker. She stopped me in the parking lot to share that her blood work had come back abnormal.

"What does that mean?" I asked.

"It's back," she said. After almost a decade in remission from cancer, she was headed to Duke Medical Center once more.

"You beat this once. I'm not worried," I said trying to provide some assurance.

"I am," she said.

"You are?" I asked, surprised by her answer. "What can I do?"

"Pray," she said. "I'm not ready."

Sherry died eight months later at Duke. She had an infection that was shutting down her organs. She was 46-years-old. She was a daughter, a mother, and one hell of a hospice social worker.

When I heard we lost Sherry, I didn't have the giant beanbag to plop down on and seek comfort. I was at home, by myself, writing this book.

I looked over at the gift from the artist now hanging in my home office. It was a sudden reminder that I didn't need a beanbag anymore. I had the words and the works of an artist, the inspiration of a life fully lived by a co-worker, and a hospice social worker who was taken too soon now comforting me.

The loss of my co-workers and my visits to the giant beenbag led me to the artist. It is the humor shared with my co-workers that reminded me laughter is the true universal language of communication. When my heart was heavy over the loss of co-workers, I recalled how important laughter in the workplace impacted me especially working in hospice. It is fond memories and laughter that inspired all the hospice staff to continue caring not only for our patients, but for each other through our own grief and loss.

I embrace the theory that "quality is so much more than quantity." The artist touched my soul. He pushed boundaries and stole a kiss. My dear friends and co-workers, Tracy, Anne, and Sherry, taken so young, taught me you never know when death will come. We must live each day as though it were our last.

"What do you do when a dying man asks for a kiss on the lips? Well ...you do it."

"To live is the rarest thing in the world. Most people just exist." —Oscar Wilde

CHAPTER NINE

Life Lesson: Wisdom trumps educational degrees.

"Educating the mind without educating the heart is no education at all." —Aristotle

My grandmother had fallen. Her arm was broken, and she required surgery. Like most elderly individuals, my grandmother claimed she had tripped, but I knew this was the beginning of the downward slope known as the end of life.

As my grandmother was coming around from anesthesia after surgery, her doctor stopped by while making his rounds. Many family members were reading, sleeping or quietly chatting in her room. It was only when the doctor came in to recap the surgery that I realized my grandmother had died in the operating room that morning.

"Good morning, everyone," the doctor began. "I want to discuss how the surgery went." Walking over to my grandmother's bed, he continued by stating, "There are a few things that you need to know."

Speaking directly to my grandmother he simply said, "You arrested on the table."

"You mean I died?" she asked, still out of sorts from the anesthesia.

"Well, your heart stopped."

"I died?" she repeated.

"Well, technically yes, but we were able to get your heart started again."

As my grandmother grabbed the doctor's hand, I was expecting her to thank him for saving her life, but that was not the case. She pulled the young doctor closer to her and asked, "Are you telling me I have to do this entire dying thing all over again?"

Many of my family members were shocked while others giggled at my grandmother's reaction. She had a knack for always making a situation unintentionally humorous. As I watched my family's responses, I turned back to stare at her, understanding for the first time that she would one day die and had no desire to do it more than once.

****

My Grandmother was affectionately called Granny by her grandchildren, but she also became known by the same name to many children in the local community. She was the matriarch of our family, the glue that held us all together. She was spunky, quick with her tongue, and a queen at the card game, UNO. She had a keen eye for killing crows that ravaged her pecan tree (pronounced pē-can) and could make you laugh at the most serious of situations.

Granny was the fourth of nine children. Her mother, my great-grandmother, was a hardworking woman. She developed a bump on her upper lip and picked at the pimple until it became infected. Blood poisoning took her life at the age of 38, leaving nine children, five still living at home.

Granny was the oldest at home and the youngest was nine months. Her four older siblings were married and building families of their own. My grandmother became the mother figure for four children—her younger sisters and one brother. It was not the life she chose, but back in those days you did what you had to do to survive.

Granny raised her sisters and brother, married, and birthed three children, one of which was still born after being carried to full term. She was married for 45 years to my grandfather and aided him through years of a paralyzing emphysema diagnosis that took his life in the late 1980s. She remarried and buried her second husband only a year after losing her family's 100-year-old farmhouse in a mysterious truck fire under the carport. These days you don't come across too many strong women like my Granny who survive the impossible without a word of complaint. She's one of the most independent individuals I ever knew.

In the spring of 2010, a year after Granny "died" during her arm surgery, I was creating another marketing element for an advance care planning program for my hospice organization called, "Begin the Conversation." The program was created to encourage individuals in the local community to begin the conversation about their own end of life desires prior to a healthcare crisis. I often worked on this project after hours and on weekends due to the overwhelming pressures of serving as Vice President of Communications and Outreach for the second largest hospice in the state of North Carolina.

I recall sitting in Granny's living room talking to her about the program when I realized she was lash-hooked to an oxygen tank. I knew in my heart she was in the last year of her life. While working in hospice care, you become very aware of the key signs of end of life. I knew it had begun, and I knew in my heart I wanted to share my knowledge about end of life.

It's ironic how wise elders always seem to have the upper hand in the end.

Granny sat next to me with my "Begin the Conversation" materials spread out before me. She was engaged in the latest reruns of the game show, "$100,000 Pyramid." Trying to redirect her attention to my hospice program, I hoped she would share some thoughts about her own death and desires for end of life planning.

I wanted to share with her that I recommended her to choose hospice. I wanted her to be comfortable and not in pain. With my position in hospice, I thought the program would be an easy sell. I convinced strangers daily about hospice care and the benefits. I knew that I could convince my grandmother to agree to hospice care to support her and my family through her final months.

Let's just say our conversation didn't go as I planned. In the end, my dear Granny provided one of biggest lesson I would learn throughout my career in working with individuals facing end of life.

As she relaxed in her recliner and watched her game show, she would occasionally peeked over at me to see what I was doing. I kept baiting her to talk about her own death.

"What do you have there?" she asked, almost breathless as she tried to speak over the slightly raised volume of the television.

"It's for work," I said confidently. "It's a program about advance care planning. "Do you know what I do, Granny?" I asked as I looked into her sweet, weak eyes.

"Yep. You kill people at the end of life," she replied without even a smirk.

She said it in a way that made me giggle because of the overshadowing myths of people's misunderstanding of what hospice care truly is, but she provided the answer she knew was correct without a doubt in her mind.

"Granny, I don't kill people at the end of life. What makes you think that?" I brazenly asked.

"You overdose them! That's what hospice is," she said.

"Granny, I work with individuals that are facing a chronic illness when treatments are not improving their quality of life," I debated, "so they can remain comfortable in their home as the disease takes its normal course. They are choosing quality over quantity. We are highly regulated by Medicare and rules that prevent us, under law, to hasten or quicken death."

My grandmother just looked at me as if, "yeah, right."

"What is the program you are working on?" She asked.

"It's called 'Begin the Conversation,'" I replied. "It helps people get in touch with how they want to face their own end of life. There is legal paperwork identifying someone to speak on your behalf when it comes to medical care if you are unable. Do you have someone like that?"

"Kathy and your father know what I want," she bluntly stated.

"Do you have the paperwork to support that?" I asked.

"We don't need no paperwork," she said with full authority in her voice.

I felt like I was eight years old with pigtails and braces. Yet, this was a clue to speak to my father, her son, about putting in place a healthcare power of attorney as well as the documents supporting her decisions.

"So, Granny, you don't want to die at home?" I asked.

"No," she sternly declared.

The next question I asked would change my life in a way that I can't even describe to this day.

"Why not, Granny?" I inquired.

"When I was a young child, families would display dead bodies for days within the farmhouse. It always scared me. I don't want my body displayed in my house after I die," she said.

"Are you okay if you die in the hospital alone in the middle of the night?" I asked with a little concern in my voice, because I did not want that for her.

"Yes, I think I am," she said.

As I pulled out of Granny's driveway, I chuckled about our conversation. Then it came to me suddenly so clearly that I had to pull my car off to the side of the road. I quickly got out, ran over to the ditch and tossed up my entire lunch into the tall weeds.

I realized for the first time in over ten years working with the dying and within hospice care, I was projecting the death I wanted for my grandmother onto her. I was trying to tell her how she should die instead of listening to how she wanted to die.

As I was throwing up on the side of Pike Road, I started to cry. It was a cry so deep it would have been called an ugly cry … but for me it was a revelation. Something inside of me wanted to turn my car around, run back into my grandmother's arms and beg for forgiveness.

On the side of Pike Road, I recalled hugging Granny tight, kissing her and telling her how much I loved her. She always told us, "When you leave, no matter for how short of time, hug the people you love, kiss them, tell them how much you love them … because you never know if you'll see them again."

I'm grateful I took her advice.

Thank goodness for Granny's forthsight to set a hospice executive for a local non-profit straight. I learned through my conversation with her that my job was not to convince individuals that hospice care was right for them, but to educate them about choices at the end of life so they can make the right choices for themselves.

That was the last conversation I ever had with my grandmother. Even though she was within weeks of her own death, she was still the matriarch of our family; the glue that held us all together. She was still spunky, quick with her tongue, and a queen at the card game, UNO. She still had a keen eye for killing crows that ravaged her pecan tree (pronounced pē-can) and could still make you laugh at the most serious of situations. She was still my Granny and my teacher, and she was dying.

I remember it clearly. It was a crisp, sunny morning in May. My house smelled clean and was prepared for a party I was hosting later that evening. At 7 a.m., my cell phone rang. It was my father. Through broken words and small deep breaths, my father told me his mother, my Granny, had passed away.

"What happened, Dad?" I asked trying to collect myself. When you hear your father crying, ever so slightly, it can bring your spirit to an immediate stop.

"She was admitted to the hospital a couple of days ago," he replied. "In Belhaven … for fluid. She was talking our ears off last night. We were laughing. We went back to her house and we got the call around 3 a.m. Her heart stopped, and she passed away. "It bothers me that she died alone in the hospital," my dad whispered with a heavy heart. A peace came over me like no other.

"Dad, let me tell you a story about my last conversation with your mother ... my Granny." Granny's voice rang true; hearing her tell me what she wanted saved me from one ounce of guilt that she died alone in the middle of the night in a hospital. I never knew how important, on multiple levels, our last conversation would be until that moment.

Since that last face to face conversation with my late grandmother, I've tried very hard not to project the death I think people should have onto them, but to listen and learn about the death they want and choose for themselves. I want to be their advocate, even if it means that an individual never experiences the wonderful care hospice can provide. It's simply not my decision. My grandmother taught me that lesson. She made me very aware of my own feelings about death and dying and made me keenly aware to never project those feelings onto other individuals.

I miss Granny tremendously. I cherish the lessons she taught me, not only at the end of her life, but throughout her life and mine.

"GRANNY"

"Live your life to the fullest
while you still can." —Unknown

CHAPTER TEN

Life Lesson: Life is a mystery.

*"The mystery of life is not a problem to be solved
but a reality to be experienced."* —*Unknown*

I learned a few things about life when I adopted a dog. Walking, peeing, and pooping were essential, basic functions. What took a bit longer to learn was that these three simple tasks would lead to a world of unexpected adventures.

My neighborhood, known as Carolina Place, is on the edge of historic downtown Wilmington. Recognized for its abundance of renowned artists, young professionals and families, the area has always been rich with culture and diversity; but admittedly has its share of occasional shady activity. Most streets steer you in the direction of Wallace Park toward its quaint bridge that takes you over Burnt Mill Creek. The bridge leads you into Forest Hills, one of the oldest neighborhoods in the city.

Having a dog in Carolina Place gave me the opportunity to meet my neighbors. Most pet owners were eager to stop and chat. We introduced ourselves, acquainted the animals, and discussed upcoming parties or how to address the latest string of car break-ins.

I made many friends as I walked Haven down the sidewalks lined with 100-year-old historic bungalows and 200-year-old trees into Wallace Park. I even found myself concerned about any neighborhood cats that scurried across 21st street by the skin of its ninth life to see if it would survive.

Regardless of rain, snow, ice, sweltering summer heat or even Atlantic hurricanes, Haven needed to walk, poop, and pee. I found friendship among the other loyal pet owners who passed me by with their own furry companions trying to accomplish the same mission.

I often came across my neighbors, Lorraine and Alan, on my treks with Haven as they walked their adopted Fox Terrier, Jerry. Lorraine was a co-worker of mine and a close friend. Alan grew up in England and moved to the United States to work as an engineer with General Electric. He was a quiet man, but would wave from afar to acknowledge us on the street as Haven and I took our regular route.

One Sunday morning, as Haven and I were headed down Metts Ave., toward Forest Hills, she was suddenly spooked. I turned around to see Alan and Jerry. I raised my hand to wave, and he did the same as he turned into his driveway and walked out of sight. I thought nothing of it and continued our walk.

Later that same evening, Haven and I headed out for an afternoon jaunt to play with her ball and run free in the park. I met a neighbor on the sidewalk who approached me with her familiar, oversized glass of white wine.

"Did you hear about Alan Perry?" Jo Ann asked.

"What do you mean?" I said. "I just saw him this morning walking his dog."

Jo Ann was obviously shaken by my response. "What do you mean you saw him this morning?" she asked as she took two huge gulps out of her full wine glass.

"He was walking Jerry. I waved at him, and he waved back. He was outside his house," I said.

"Alan died five days ago" Jo Ann replied.

"What?" I asked, trying to comprehend what Jo Ann was saying.

"Alan died," she reiterated.

"What?" I asked again, "but I just saw him this morning."

As Jo Ann took another huge swallow out of her wine glass, I asked, "Can I have a sip of that?"

****

Lorraine and Alan Perry were married for 26 years. She spent many years working for the oncology healing arts department at a local Wilmington hospital. Wanting more out of her career, Lorraine went back to school to obtain her master's degree so she could work in the field of hospice care.

Knowing that an internship was required to complete her coursework, Lorraine set her sights on England and applied to St. Christopher's Hospice, the oldest modern hospice facility in existence. It made sense. Alan was from England, the kids were grown, and it would be a new adventure for the couple.

St. Christopher's was founded by Dame Cecily Saunders in 1967. As a trained nurse, medical social worker and physician, she was involved with terminally ill patients as far back as 1948. Dame Cecily revolutionized how to care for the ill, the dying and the bereaved. Establishing her own home as a sanctuary for the dying, she welcomed patients and staff from all faiths to include believers and non-believers. Her own strong sense of Christian faith was a fundamental factor in her commitment to the dying and was an anchor throughout her life as she uncompromisingly laid the groundwork for modern day hospice care initiatives.

Lorraine applied to St. Christopher's and was invited for a formal interview. As she sat in the lobby, the head administrator introduced herself and said to Lorraine, "All International students are required to be interviewed by Dame Cecily."

Flabbergasted, Lorraine blurted out, "I thought she died!"

"No," said the British administrator as she tried not to laugh, "She's very much alive."

Lorraine was then led into the lunch hall of St. Christopher's to be interviewed by Dame Cecily "The Legendary" Saunders. She immediately noticed the double-breasted pinstriped suit paired with a starched white blouse and sensible shoes.

"How did this entire movement start?" Lorraine asked the broad-shouldered, stately woman. "It's a very long story, but to keep time I'll give you the highlights as best I can remember." Dame Saunders stated.

"My father was getting older," she began. "I was a social worker and a nurse, and I later became a physician. I started to look for social engagements to help entertain my father and his friends. They were all World War II veterans and had lost their wives. I could not find anything suitable for them. Every place we visited was limited because of medical restrictions. My father would not have that. He wanted to enjoy his last years with pleasures."

"With pleasures," Lorraine acknowledged.

"Yes, pleasures," the Dame continued. "He wanted to have his cocktails, play cards, tend to his greenhouse, and play cricket. He wanted to sit in his art or music room in front of the fire and tell old war stories. My husband and I could not find a place that would allow him and his friends such pleasures."

"One evening my husband and I were discussing what to do with a huge house we owned in south London. It came to mind to bring my father and his friends there to provide for them and create something that would allow them to feel they were still living."

In complete awe of the perceived ghost sitting in front of her, Lorraine knew she was being told the story of how the first modern day hospice began. She was mesmerized by how the Dame's stethoscope was still hanging around her neck during lunch and the entire conversation.

There was a pause.

"So, tell me about you," Dame Cecily inquired.

Lorraine took some time to tell the "Legendary" Saunders about herself. She spoke to the

Dame about her husband, Alan, and what southeastern North Carolina meant to her as a home.

"I have visited southern states," Dame Cecily stated. "What I found out about you Yanks is that you are such a curative bunch."

"Why wouldn't we try to cure?" Lorraine asked, just coming from an oncologist floor in an acute-care hospital.

"Well my dear, we are a very small island, and we can't keep everyone alive."

Lorraine contemplated the Dame's words but kept her thoughts to herself. Silently she asked herself, "What does that have to do with anything?" Suddenly she realized, however, that the conversation was opening her eyes to a different perspective. She was face to face with a woman who was suggesting she think about death and dying in a whole different way.

Within a few moments, Dame Cecily looked at Lorraine and said, "You're a go."

The internship went along brilliantly for about eight months, but two days before Christmas, Lorraine found Alan suffering from paralysis on the right side of his face. Amid experiencing socialized medicine in a different country and unlearning the American way to view death, Lorraine found herself coping with her own family crisis.

Alan was admitted to the hospital, and it was determined that he had officially experienced a stroke. A robust British nurse soon bobbed into his room with much authority and demanded that Alan's smoking days were over. Allen had been a smoker for much of his life. Lorraine leaned over his bed and asked, "Are you sure you understand what the nurse just ordered?" Alan only nodded, because he could not speak. She left for home and purged the house of all cigarettes, ashtrays, and lighters.

While Lorraine continued to work at St. Christopher's, Alan worked hard to learn to speak and write again. Within a very short time, his motor skills and mobility had return. One of his doctors related to him, "You have an average IQ. You have made a full recovery, sir."

"I've never had an average IQ," he said. "It has always been above average."

"Well, for most people, average is good enough," the doctor quipped.

Although Alan physically recovered from his stroke, in many ways he was unable to emotionally recover. He became more reserved and self-conscious of his slightly altered speech.

When Lorraine's internship ended, she and Alan returned to their home in Wilmington, NC. I sometimes ran into Alan as he walked his dog, Jerry, and noticed that he had become less talkative. He still engaged with his occasional wave of acknowledgement and listened to me ramble at times while Jerry and Haven interacted.

After arriving home from England, Lorraine started working full-time with our local hospice. As a volunteer, she created a healing arts program on a zero-budget based upon her belief that the arts were a vital part of hospice care. She implemented many ideas she learned at St. Christopher's into our local program, and begged and borrowed from anyone to create one of the leading healing arts programs on the coast of North Carolina.

Many years later, Alan was suddenly diagnosed with tongue cancer that eventually metastasized to his kidneys. Maintaining his usual stoic English manner, he never complained, but he became even more reclusive.

After major surgery to remove the cancer from his kidneys, one of his doctors advised the couple there was nothing more to worry about. Lorraine and Alan put faith in his words and moved forward with their lives without a second glance back. Alan seemed to be feeling great, or according to Lorraine, he wasn't complaining. The couple was confident they had passed the test and beat the cancer.

As the North Carolina Azalea Festival approached, their neighbors were preparing to host a portion of the garden tour at their home. Alan was concerned that guests would be peeping over the fence line and wanted their own yard in pristine condition for the festivities. He and Lorraine, much to her chagrin, spent a full day raking, cutting branches, edging the lawn, and trimming bushes.

Lorraine often recalls that last Sunday in the yard. As Alan raked the last pile of leaves into a plastic bag, their daughter-in-law, Abby, and their grandson stopped by for a visit. Offering to take the bags of gathered debris to the curb, Lorraine thought to herself that she could not remember the last time Abby had offered to help with manual labor, but she must have seen how exhausted the couple was after their day's work. In hindsight, Lorraine should have known something was upon them, but she was in complete denial. Through all her years working with individuals at the end of their life, Lorraine did not recognize that Alan was experiencing his last moments. It wasn't until his last hours that she understood she was losing him.

After finishing the yard on Sunday, Alan was tired and went to lie down. The next morning, Lorraine prepared breakfast and left for work only to find his food untouched when she arrived home. Monday evening, as Lorraine tried to assist Allen to the bathroom, she noticed some mottling at his feet, a common skin discolorization that occurs prior to death. She knew something was wrong on some level, but she could not face the reality that Alan was dying.

At 3 a.m. Tuesday morning, Lorraine knew what was happening. As the couple laid in bed together, she began to cry. Alan put his arm around her and said, "Everything is going to be okay."

"No, Alan, it's not. You're dying," she replied.

"I know," he answered. "And everything is going to be okay."

"I'm so sorry for yelling at you yesterday," she replied

"You did nothing wrong," he said to her as he pulled her in closer.

By 6 a.m., Lorraine had called a close friend and hospice nurse. She put in a referral and the hospice admission nurse arrived at 8 a.m. Alan died shortly before noon, prior to being admitted to hospice.

A few days later, Lorraine asked her daughter-in-law, Abby, if she knew Alan was dying that day in the yard. "I just knew something didn't seem right," she replied.

The following Sunday, Lorraine's cousin hosted a morning breakfast to celebrate Alan's life. At noon, she pulled out the shot glasses for family and friends to pay tribute to Alan with a final toast. It wasn't important if those attending didn't like Guinness, all that mattered was that Alan did.

It was that same Sunday morning that Haven and I headed down Metts Ave., toward Forest Hills, when she was suddenly spooked. I turned around to see Alan and Jerry. I raised my hand to wave, and I saw him wave back as he turned into his driveway and walked out of sight.

Life is a mystery. I can only tell you what I saw and experienced that day when I knew nothing about Alan's passing several days earlier. When Lorraine returned to work, I sat down and told her my story. I hoped it would not cause her more pain, but I also hoped she would see the mystery of life.

And she did.

"I raised my hand to wave, and he did the same as he turned into his driveway and walked out of sight."

"If you change the way you look at things,
the things you look at change." Wayne Dyer

CHAPTER ELEVEN

Life Lesson: Perspective can change based on your viewpoint.

"There are things known and there are things unknown, and in between are the doors of perception." Aldous Huxley

In the movie "Dead Poet's Society," the late Robin Williams' character, Mr. Keating, teaches us many valuable life lessons throughout the entire film. There is a scene in which Mr. Keating is talking to his students about poetry and suddenly jumps on top of his desk. He asks them, "Why do I stand on my desk?"

"To be taller," Mr. Dalton quickly responds.

With his foot, Mr. Keating rings a bell. "Nope," he says, "but thanks for playing. I stand upon my desk to consistently remind myself to look at things in a different way."

As he turns in a circle to look around the room and ponder the different views, he profoundly states, "The world looks different from up here. You don't believe me? Come see for yourself." He encourages all the boys to join him on this exploration of seeing things from a different perspective.

As the boys walk toward the front of the class, Mr. Keating continues, "Just when you think you know something, you have to look at it in another way. Even though it may seem silly or wrong, you must try. You must strive to find your own voice, but the longer you wait to begin, the less likely you are to find it at all."

Norma Bauerschmidt understood Mr. Keating's philosophy about new perspectives, Miss Norma was a 90-year-old who refused aggressive treatment for her cancer to experience a new perspective on living. She taught me that it is never too late to say, "yes" to living.

By changing perspectives, you can change the world. New perspectives can help you relate to individuals you never would have considered to be a friend. They allow you the capability to look into the eyes of a 5-year-old child leaning into the unknown and encourage you to ask for what you want. Different viewpoints can change just about anything, including how you look at death, mortality, and the journey of life.

Have you ever changed your perspective to see something or someone differently?

Remember when your grandparents or parents reminded you to look at a situation through someone else's eyes or walk in their shoes before you judge? Many times we consciously avoid stepping up on a desk to look around at all the different viewpoints, but life has a funny way of forcing us to see things differently from time to time.

****

As a non-clinical, creative young professional working in a seasoned clinical environment, I understood that knowledge would be a key factor in proving to myself and the clinical staff that I could be a trusted leader. I became a student of end of life care, and even read the entire "Medicare Conditions of Participation for Hospice Care" manuscript. I wondered how the government could be so vague in their dissertation. From the creative side, I found loopholes throughout the documents that allowed a sliver of room for hospice organizations to care for people facing end of life instead of treating them like steel widgets.

I found it interesting how creative and clinical staff working together could unknowingly work against each other to interrupt the eligibility of an individual to enter hospice care under the Medicare benefit. Of course, I wanted to push the limits and rebel against the conservative checklist to meet individual's needs. It never turns out well when a senior leader is okay with paying Medicare back based on that ever so gray line between patient and family eligibility or non-eligibility.

In my effort to challenge government guidelines and educate myself, I began to read medical journals, follow "The New York Times," and build relationships with people at the National Hospice and Palliative Care Organization (NHPCO). On a different scale, I took the time to relate to our small clinical staff on a personal basis. I interacted with them as people instead of categorizing each by their job title. I would often make copies of relevant, interesting articles, and provide them to the staff based on their role within the organization.

If you're a salesperson, you must know everything about your product. I became the epitome of a salesperson. I became hugely arrogant and all-knowing but very passionate about my job. I had colossal goals to meet in my position, and desired respect from the clinicians. Failure to succeed was not an option.

Interoffice catchphrases became "Increase the Census," "Bring in More Referrals," and "Hospice is the Right Choice for Everyone Facing a Serious Illness." My colleagues encouraged these in-house slogans, and I bought into them all. My arrogance and inexperience made me question the choices of families and patients. I wondered why they would ever choose aggressive treatment over hospice care. I was on a balancing beam armed with knowledge, but I lacked a true understanding of the dynamics that impacted everyone and everything that had to do with death and dying.

Then life forced a perspective change on me that I could not ignore. It was the spring of 2008, and I had just adopted a puppy. I named her Bella. She was a Chow/Something mix that was nothing but a ball of black fur with the pinkest tongue and sweetest personality you've ever met.

After three weeks, just as Bella and I were finally adapting to a routine, she became lethargic and stopped eating. Within 24 hours, she was vomiting and had severe diarrhea. It was a long ride to the vet for both of us.

The doctor took us back immediately and began to take vitals, do blood work, and perform several other tests. As I waited for the results, I held my precious 10-pound Bella in my arms and cried, because I was afraid of what the test results would reveal.

After a long wait, the doctor came back in to the room and said, "It's Parvo."

"What is Parvo?" I asked.

"Canine Parvovirus is a highly contagious virus that can affect all dogs, but unvaccinated dogs and puppies younger than four months old are the most at risk. The virus affects dogs' gastrointestinal tracts and is spread by direct dog-to-dog contact. Most deaths from Parvo occur within 48 to 72 hours following the onset of clinical signs if not treated." The look on the veterinarian's face was grim.

"She's going to die." I said.

"It doesn't look good, but let's take one day at a time," the vet said with a glimmer of hope in her voice.

Before I knew it, I had placed my weak Bella on the table in front of the vet. "Save her, Doctor," I pleaded. "Do whatever you have to do to save her. No matter how much it costs, not matter how much it takes ... save this dog!"

"We will do all we can," she said.

As I watched the vet take Bella back into the clinic, I gathered my things and walked out of the office without my little girl. Tears were streaming down my face when I suddenly stopped in my tracks. I asked myself, "Is this what families feel when they receive a life-threatening diagnosis for someone they love?"

My words to the doctor kept coming back to me. "Save this dog no matter the cost. Do what you have to do to save her." I sat in my car, completely overwhelmed and worried about Bella, but my perspective had completely changed. I was horrified that I had never considered the other side of a diagnosis when it came to marketing hospice care.

It took ten days for Bella to recover, but I was forever changed. From that moment on, I never created another hospice marketing campaign without considering how the message would be received in the eyes of a patient and in the heart of a family member.

Each time I've been 100 percent committed to an end of life issue, life seemed to slap me in the face with an up close and personal experience that ultimately changed my perspective. After reading Atul Gwande's book, *Being Mortal*, I realized that our medical culture is not about putting what matters most to patients first but about aggressively treating those with debilitating diseases. There were so many topics Dr. Gwande addressed in his book that I agreed with that I felt it was a love song to all baby boomers destined to enter the world of Medicare healthcare.

One excerpt from his book was tattooed and permanently engraved on my heart. It reads:

"If seriously ill patients in their 80s end up in the ICU of our local hospitals, the healthcare professionals and the system itself have failed them in every way possible."
-Atul Gwande.

I found that statement to be so true and have used it in many presentations. I used it to empower my community to voice what they desired at end of life, so if they did end up in ICU, it was their personal choice and not lack of knowledge.

****

I traveled to Winston-Salem in June of 2015 for a speaking engagement to present the topic of how clinical professionals could creatively open the door to difficult conversations with their patients about advance care planning. My great aunt, Doris, happened to be flying in to Raleigh, and I planned an overnight stay with her prior to my presentation in Winston-Salem the next day.

Upon my arrival to the townhouse located just north of Raleigh in Wakefield, several family members were milling around outside. As I embraced my cousins, Ed and Teresa, I saw an elderly lady feebly walk around the corner. It was Aunt Doris.

It had been almost a year since I had seen her in her hometown of Venice, FL. I noticed she had aged, on that visit south, but she still had that youthful spirit in her that I remembered as a child. The woman walking toward me that day in Raleigh had no youthful spirit, was unstable on her feet, and had lost a dramatic amount of weight. As I put my arms around her and told her I loved her, I could feel she was nothing but skin and bones.

Breaking our embrace and holding back tears I stated, "I'm going to make a drink." I was overwhelmed by the difference that a year had made in the appearance of my dear Aunt Doris. She was like a mother to me. She knew my imperfections and loved me unconditionally. I felt at times like I was the fifth child among her children Tony, Teresa, Tana, and Ed.

I walked through the patio, entered the house and closed the back door behind me. I could not hold back the tears. I knew that this was the last year of Aunt Doris' life. I was looking into the eyes of one of our hospice patients. I slowly walked to the fridge, put ice in a glass and started to pour a stiff drink just as Teresa came in to refill her own glass.

"I'm glad you could come," said Teresa. "It means a lot to Mom." She did not notice my tears as she refreshed her cocktail. I turned away from her to wipe my face.

"You okay?" She asked.

"Of course, it is great to see your mom and just be here," I said.

"What's the matter?" Teresa pressed, knowing me well enough to know when something was bothering me.

I turned toward her and said, "Your mother will never live to see your son's wedding in June."

"What?" She asked.

"I've seen the look in so many hospice patient's eyes, and your mother will not be here in a year," I said with conviction.

"Stop it. What are you saying? She is fine." Finally noticing my tears, she asked, "You're serious?"

"She is sick, Teresa," I said.

Teresa hugged me and emphatically said with her usual positive spin on things, "Well, she is here today."

Two days later I received a frantic call from Teresa. "Mom passed out in the parking lot of a shopping mall!"

A two-week vacation for Aunt Doris had turned into a month that included multiple hospitalizations, small procedures, and a fall that broke her hip. With each hospitalization, Aunt Doris looked older and more fragile. She was eating like a bird and having complications with breathing. It was now September, and the time had come to consider moving her to Raleigh.

Only days prior to moving into her new apartment with Teresa, Aunt Doris had another setback and was headed back to the hospital one last time. On November 11th, after several days in the hospital, her heart stopped. The doctors revived her, and the nurses began calling in the family.

Tana and Teresa, her two daughters, arrived first. As each of them tended to their mother on either side of the bed, Aunt Doris asked, "Is Tony coming?"

"Yes, Mom," Teresa said. "He's on his way."

"I'm so sorry," Aunt Doris said as she tightly gripped her daughters' hands.

"Mom, it's okay," Tana replied as she brushed her mom's hair back away from her face.

Those would be the last words Aunt Doris would speak.

I was standing in the workroom at my hospice organization when I received the call.

"Hey Teresa, what's up? I'm really late to a Veteran's event,"I said.

"It's Mom." Teresa's voice was not the same cheery voice I was used to hearing over the phone.

"What's wrong?" I asked.

"I don't think Mom is going to make it through the day," Teresa said in a quivering voice.

"We've been asked to call family in."

"Where is she?" I asked.

"She is in the cardiac ICU at WakeMed," Teresa said.

"I'm on my way," I replied, then reiterated, "I'm on my way."

It was a two-hour drive from Wilmington to Raleigh. I raced home, dumped a few things in a bag, dropped the dog off in a panic and started racing down I-40 toward the cardiac ICU at WakeMed Health. Looking back, I don't even recall driving. I knew Aunt Doris would not be with us in a year, but hearing the news that she was actively dying put even this seasoned hospice professional in shock. I took off without telling anyone.

When I arrived at the hospital, I walked up to the help desk and frantically requested guidance to the cardiac ICU wing. A volunteer offered to take me so I wouldn't get lost. It felt like it took weeks to reach the ICU. As the double doors opened, Ed motioned me back to the room.

I had made it in time. Aunt Doris lay in the bed with labored breathing as the machines beeped around her. She was surrounded by nurses coming in and out of the room, but she was also enveloped by the people she loved and those who loved her. When I approached her bed, I grabbed her hand, kissed her forehead, and whispered, "I'm here. Everything is going to be okay. I'm here."

My heart was breaking. My great Aunt Doris was the one McKinney sister that truly knew me. She favored my Granny and was the dying mother of my best friend. I felt helpless, confused, and in complete shock.

I had just begun the chapter titled, "Don't Die in the Hospital," but there I was in a hospital room surrounded by the people who matter most to me. We were coming to the edge of death, and all of us knew we couldn't go with Aunt Doris. The chapter name changed to "Perceptive can Change Based on Your Point of View," because when my viewpoint changed so did my opinion.

After releasing her hand, I hugged each of my family members and positioned myself at the foot of her bed. I placed a hand on her leg under the warm blanket.   I just sat there and listened to Aunt Doris' grandson tell her how much he loved her through his tears. I heard Tana tell her mother how much she loved her and witnessed Teresa and Tony embrace at the window. I grabbed Ed's hand as he stood beside me at the foot of bed.

There I sat in the middle of an ICU hospital room at one of the largest hospitals in Raleigh. I heard the beeps and noticed the nursing staff rush in and out of the room, but the most important thing I saw was seven individuals crowded in that room who stopped their worlds to rush to Aunt Doris' bedside.

The beeps indicated a decline in blood pressure and heart rate. They would get faster as Aunt Doris' vital signs dropped. I hated the beeps. Just when I wanted to tell the staff to turn off the machines, I felt something like a breeze. It was almost as if someone had taken a piece of paper and fanned me. I looked around the room to see if anyone else had noticed it. Still at the foot of the bed, I felt a slight breeze again. As soon as it passed, the beeps became faster. Again, I looked around to see if anyone else was feeling this, but no one seemed to notice. The beeps became faster and I felt another breeze. My Aunt Doris suddenly sat up in the bed, reached her hand out as if to grab something and took her last breath. As her body slowly relaxed into the bed, her arm fell to her side.

A reverent silence came over the room. The breeze was gone. A doctor came in, listened to her heart and confirmed, "She is no longer with us." And just like that, my Aunt Doris was gone. Several of my family members were laying on her, some were holding her hands, while others were telling her they loved her when something occurred to me.

I looked at each person within that room. They had raced from work, left things undone, and dropped everything to be with Aunt Doris. They didn't race to her side because she was dying; they raced to her side because of how she had lived. There I sat in an ICU hospital room watching one of the most important people in my life leave this world. It was horrible. It was beautiful. Death can be one of the most beautiful experiences in life if you are able to be at the bedside of someone you love and support them through the transition to their next great adventure.

As my family and I gathered our things and walked toward the door, I glanced back to Aunt Doris' spiritless body one last time. It was hard to walk away from the physicality that we as humans need from our loved ones and to embrace the energy left behind, but

Aunt Doris' spirit remains with all of us.

Do I think dying in the ICU is right for me? No, but I can't see into the future or predict the happenings that may occur to bring me to the edge of death within a hospital room.

My perspective on dying in the ICU changed that day. It is not where you die, but who is with you when you die that trumps everything. Thinking of my own death, I pray I'm lucky enough to have people surround my bed, tell me how much they love me, thank me for how much I meant to them, and forgive me for all my crazy imperfections. In the end, I hope that they show up and hold my hand no matter where I may be.

"Just when you think you know something, you have to look at it in another way," Mr. Keating preached. I would tend to agree with you, Mr. Keating. Changing your perspective can change the world and assist you in finding your own voice especially at the end of life.

"Just when you think you know something, you have to look at it in another way," Mr. Keating preached.

"As a human being, I'm a work in progress."
—John Lydon

CHAPTER TWELVE

Life Lesson: Physicians are not God, they're just human.

"A good physician treats the disease; the great physician treats the patient who has the disease." —William Osler

There were days when I loved working with physicians, but there were also days when I hid from them and even questioned the motives behind their recommendations for curative treatment of their dying patients. Within our healthcare culture and disease management system, I witnessed how some doctor's methods were based on the shape and scope of their personal practice goals rather than the needs of their patients. There were times it seemed that some medical decisions were driven by a practitioner's desire to enhance their bottom line.

In a fee-for-service healthcare industry, no one wins, especially patients and their families who are facing a serious illness or death. Late referrals, over-treatment, and deliveries of false hope at end of life only led to additional suffering for patients and their loved ones.

I saw patients being herded through our non-inclusive healthcare system who were bewildered and confused by treatment options and unrealistic expectations. There were many times doctors ordered treatment on their own accord or allowed treatment at the request of a patient or family member that did more harm than good and lessened the quality of life for a patient in their final days.

I interviewed many physicians and researched hospice referral patterns during my tenure, and I learned two important facts. I first found that doctors were not extensively trained in medical school to have frank, difficult conversations with their patients at end of life. Although I did find positive progress in curriculum at many schools that focused on delivering bad news to patients who were terminally ill, I also found that when young medical students were put in an acute setting, their older counterparts applied pressure to unlearn the new, innovative techniques they had been taught. The new doctors were directed by their senior practicing physicians to do it their way or take the highway.

The second important fact I discovered during my interviews and research was that there is a human side to physicians that takes them beyond their training. Most physicians generally don't want to fail their patients, but for some of them, ego and income sometimes affect their decisions about treatment. After working in the hospice industry, I realized that many healthcare providers often knew that end of life treatments would not extend a patient's life, so why would they continue to offer them? It should be up to the patient and their family members, the consumers, to determine what is in their best interest for quality of life, dying, and death.

During that last year at hospice, I remember sitting at my desk working on another marketing campaign. I had no idea it would be the last one I would create for the organization. One of our medical directors walked into my office with such a defeated look on her face. I was keenly aware that she was having a very bad day.

"Are you okay, Dr. Kristen?" I immediately asked.

"I'm not sure I can continue working here," she said as she sat down in front of me.

I became close with several of our medical directors. We often discussed articles featured in the Journal of the American Medical Association (JAMA) and talked about new programs to enhance non-medical care at end of life.

So there sat Dr. Kristen in front of my desk. She was my doctor friend who brought me homemade tea each week as we discussed spirituality's impact on our daily lives at hospice. That day was different. The cheery medical director that I knew looked completely wounded and deflated.

"I can't do this anymore," she said with so much conviction that I thought she had already resigned.

"If you go, I go," I said without skipping a beat. "You look like you've been in a street fight."

"I have," she said. "I don't think we will ever get our message through to the medical community when it comes to the benefits of hospice and palliative care for their seriously ill patients. They just don't get it."

"I've been here so long," she continued, "but I can't change the mindset of our local oncologists. I just don't understand how they can't recognize a dying patient."

"What in the world happened?" I asked.

"We received a referral from Dr. Wilde," she said.

Dr. Wilde was one of our top referral sources and actively involved in our hospice program on many levels, but it was a flip of a coin on any given day to figure out if you were communicating with Dr. Jekyll or Mr. Hyde.

"He had a patient at his office that he wanted to transfer over to our hospice care center," Dr. Kristen continued, "but he gave the patient a $15,000 round of chemotherapy this morning."

"What?" I asked. "So, if the patient was being referred to hospice, why did he give him an aggressive chemo treatment?"

"That's the million-dollar question," she replied. "We couldn't admit the patient to the hospice care center because we were full, and we can't admit and bill on the same day a patient receives aggressive treatment."

Basically what Dr. Kristen was telling me was that we had no beds at our care center, our medical director could not admit the patient because of double-billing through Medicare, and Dr. Wilde was not happy.

"In fact," Dr. Kristen said, "Dr. Wilde is downright pissed off."

I was often notified when physicians were upset with our hospice services. It was part of my job to oversee the provider outreach department and provide continued education to doctor's offices. The outreach department's goal was to maintain key relationships with physicians and address any issues regarding service delivery to providers and patients. Our provider outreach liaison, Sara, just happened to be with Dr. Wilde to assist with his referral when he lost his temper. By the time Sara left the oncologist's office, she had been verbally abused.

"Poor Sara," Dr. Kristen continued. "She really got a lashing from Dr. Wilde. He was hysterical, screaming at her and then yelling at our medical director at our care center over the phone. I tried to help, but he yelled and hung up on me."

"Why was he was so upset?" I asked.

"I assume he made a promise to the family that once they received the chemo treatment the patient would get a bed at the care center," she said.

"Oops," I responded.

"We scheduled an admission later in the evening to home hospice and reassured everyone, the patient would be transferred to the care center when a bed became available," she said.

"Sounds reasonable," I said.

"When the hospice admission nurse arrived to admit the patient," Dr. Kristen continued, "he was in a cardiac episode. There were no documents supporting the patient's wishes, so our hospice nurse had to perform CPR. She could not revive him."

There was a long pause as we both stared at each other.

"Are you thinking what I'm thinking?" I asked.

"Dr. Wilde killed that patient," she said with conviction. "And he made thousands of dollars off that last chemotherapy treatment."

"Maybe the patient wanted the treatment?" I asked, hoping there was some logical reason why this situation had occurred.

"Doctors take an oath to do no harm," she firmly stated. "What Dr. Wilde did was wrong."

"You should call and talk to him," I said.

"What?" she said. "If I did that, I would never be able to work in this town again. That is why I ask myself if I can continue to do this when I see things like this happening every week."

A tear fell down Dr. Kristen's face. She still looked defeated and bewildered.

As she walked out of my office, I wanted to scream. I could not believe that she felt so powerless and afraid, but I knew that she was right. When you live in a small community, especially a small medical community, holding other physicians accountable for their actions, right or wrong, was strongly frowned upon.

As I shut down my computer, I realized that everyone had lost in this situation. Dr. Kristen had struggled to care for an actively dying patient upon referral. Sara, our hospice liaison, had been verbally abused for doing her job. Our medical director had to listen to the rants of Dr. Wilde as well. At the end of the day it was the patient and family who lost the most. I wondered if Dr. Wilde felt like he lost something that day too.

Driving home that evening, I asked myself several questions.

Did the patient want to receive this last dose of chemo knowing it would not prolong his life?

Did anyone explain the pros and cons of the treatment to the patient and his family before it was administered?

What was the physician thinking? Did he know the patient personally?

Was he a neighborhood friend who knew the family? Was he trying to do everything possible to assist the patient and the caregivers to give them one more day together?

Was the doctor upholding the AMA's code of ethics to "Do No Harm?"

What was the physician's motivation in providing unnecessary treatment to an actively dying patient?

If the patient was not actively dying, did the $15,000 chemo-therapy treatment lead to his demise?

I had no interest in being judge and jury that day, but I had to ask myself those questions. My job was to empower others to ask those same questions. People forget that physicians are not God. They are mortal human beings, just like the rest of us. As I contemplated the human condition of our doctors on my drive home, I began to widen my perspective on their jobs at hand.

What if ...

Dr. Wilde had an emotional connection with his patient?

The patient and his family requested the chemo treatment, and the physician reluctantly agreed, knowing there was nothing else that could be done?

The doctor explained all the risks involved, and the family still insisted that they go ahead with the treatment?

Did the physician's ego get in the way of his decision-making process, and he saw an opportunity to profit from a dying man?

Any one of these scenarios would prove that Dr. Wilde is very human.

Dr. Kristen and I never learned the details of what happened between Dr. Wilde and his patient that day, because we were not in the room. Neither one of us was inside the mind of the physician when he made the decisions that he did. Third party information was unreliable, because perceptions from outsiders were only opinions.

The whole experience reiterated the ugly truth about our healthcare system. I knew that it had become just a business. It was just another example of how bedside manner had turned into high productivity through advanced science that only led to higher profit margins. It forced me to question how our medical industry could advance so quickly in acute care settings while at the same time give little or no benefit to those facing end of life. Had it become ethical to allow patients with serious illnesses to live their final days in prolonged suffering? What had become of "Do No Harm?"

****

On the eve of completing what I thought would be the final chapter of my book, I received a call from my father. As I answered the phone, he frankly said, "I'm having some issues with lymphoma."

No matter how long you work in hospice or palliative care, when your father calls to tell you he has a life-threatening illness it will stop you in your tracks and shake the very core of your foundation.

"What does this mean?" I asked in shock.

"I had a little skin issue on my forehead," he continued. "The doctor thought after looking at it that I needed a PET scan. He found some spots on one of my lungs. He plans to do a couple of biopsies to confirm."

"How do you feel?" I asked.

"I feel fine," he replied.

"Well, Dad," I started, mustering all my courage to even speak. "We are all dying. No one is guaranteed tomorrow. Let's take this one day at a time. Let's confirm the diagnosis and hear what your doctors recommend."

"Yep, no one is guaranteed tomorrow," he agreed. "That is for sure."

"Don't misunderstand me, Dad," I said with a quivering voice. "I might cry later tonight, but I'm a little bit in shock right now."

"Me too," was all he could say.

The next two weeks felt like two months. I could not write or really think about anything else. I forced myself to imagine a world without my father, and the visions were painful and scary.

I called my father the morning he was scheduled to have two biopsies taken from his lung and bone marrow. The doctor was so confident that his biopsies would come back malignant that he arranged for a surgeon to put in a port for chemotherapy while he was under anesthesia to avoid another invasive procedure prior to cancer treatments.

Dad had suffered from Rheumatoid Arthritis for 25 years, but he lived a pretty normal life due to advanced treatment. The powerful medication he was prescribed caused major skin irritations that left open wounds on his arms and forehead. In 2015, small bumps on each arm turned into massive wounds the size of softballs on both elbows. You could see down to the bone. Surgery seemed inevitable until his doctor took him off his arthritis medicine. Within weeks, the wounds on both arms healed on their own.

When my father and stepmother went to the oncologist's office to get the results of his biopsies, the doctor looked at the outcome and was surprised. "I've seen cases very similar to yours," he said looking up from his paperwork toward my father. "Lymphoma is a concern with arthritic patients, but I'm fortunate to tell you that you do not have cancer."

My father called that afternoon, and as I answered the phone, he frankly said, "I don't have cancer."

"What?" I asked. I was riding a roller coaster of emotions.

"I don't have cancer," he emphatically said again.

"But they inserted a port for chemo, Dad," I blurted out in bewilderment. "Why would they do that if they weren't sure?" I was suddenly livid with the doctor. My father had gone through an invasive, unnecessary procedure based on assumptions instead of facts. It was just another example of how our healthcare system jumps the gun to over treat patients prior to confirming a diagnosis.

Then I suddenly stopped. I felt relief. My father did not have cancer.

I had to reflect on the humanity of his oncologist who had seen test results come back time after time with a cancer diagnosis for his patients. He did assume, but this time he was wrong. I began to empathize with his doctor. I put myself in his shoes and something unexpected happened. I started to wonder about all the patients and families he had to look in the eye and say, "You have cancer."

What a rare moment that must have been for him to look my father in the eye and say, "You don't have cancer." He was human. He assumed the worst, but his intentions were good. He was preparing my father for treatments. Dad was one of the lucky ones. My father did not have cancer.

Dad's misdiagnosis reminded me that most physicians, nurses, and other healthcare providers do their best to treat and enhance quality of life. They make mistakes like all of us do; they are human too. In this case, their intentions were good.

"DAD"

"Courage is not the absence of fear but the acquired ability to move beyond fear." – Matthew Kelly

CHAPTER THIRTEEN

Life Lesson: Trust your gut.
It is the best compass we have.

"Trust your vibes. Energy doesn't lie." —Unknown

Trusting oneself is a hard lesson to learn. Numerous times in my life I noticed my gut telling me something, ignored it, and then found myself regretting it later.

I always had gut feelings, but it was only after working with individuals facing end of life that I learned to have faith in them. Once I started trusting my intuition, I witnessed many wondrous things happen throughout my career.

You know what I'm talking about. It's that little feeling deep down in your stomach that warns you of danger, pulls you away from something, and stops you in your tracks to take pause and listen. It can urge you to take a leap of faith or impel you to take a risk to do something totally unrealistic. At times, if you let its magnetism pull you in, your friends and family may question your sanity. Your gut is something you can't ignore. You must take the leap and come face to face with your own potential insecurities.

I met a lot of individuals through the years who ignored their gut feeling and trusted doctors in order to avoid their fear of dying. They never had the opportunity to lean into the wonderment, beauty, and mystery of death. I also met many people along the way who trusted their inner voice, believed in a higher power, and walked through their finals days embracing love and the gift of life in its present moment.

It was a beautiful spring day when we received a referral to assist a five-year old girl in an adjacent county. Young children referrals were always hard, because many parents cannot come to terms with the reality of their child's impending death. They can't get past the point of trying to do everything possible to provide a quality, pain-free, cancer-free childhood for their kids. No parent wants to or should endure the pain of burying a child.

I received a phone call from the hospice nurse assigned to the five-year-old asking me to bring some extra supplies from our local hospital's pediatric department. Without hesitation, I rushed out the door, picked up the supplies and began my 35-minute commute to the family's house.

I took a deep breath before I knocked on the door. When it opened, a young woman stood in front of me. She wasn't much older than me, but I could see that grief had aged her.

"Are you from hospice?" she asked with an exhausted look on her face.

"Yes, Joan requested a few additional supplies," I replied.

"Come in," she said. "She is with Faith in her room. Follow me."

As I walked down the hallway, I could hear laughter from a small child. As I entered the doorway, I found our hospice nurse sitting on the floor stacking blocks with the most beautiful 5-year old girl I had ever seen. Her long curly blonde hair fell down her back. Her emerald green eyes and laughter immediately made me smile. Only when she looked up did I notice the feeding tube in her right nostril.

"Who are you?" she asked.

"I'm here to bring you some things that might help you," I said.

As Joan inventoried the supplies, she turned to the little girl and asked, "Are you ready to change your dressing?"

"No ... blocks," she demanded.

"Miss Kimberly will play with you while I go see Mommy and Daddy," she said as she motioned me toward the child. "I'll be right back."

As I sat down next to her, those tender green eyes met with mine. "Stack them," she said. Before I could even wrap my mind around the fact that this little miracle was in hospice care, I began stacking blocks. As soon as they were high enough, she knocked them down and rocked back in an explosion of laughter.

"Again," she said.

After several stacks were demolished, Joan walked back in and bent down to Faith. "Are you ready?" she asked.

"Yes," Faith replied.

I started cleaning the pile of blocks scattered around the room. Joan placed Faith on a changing table and started undressing her. Out of the blue, I heard the most powerful question I'd ever heard a child ask. "Am I dying?" She asked.

I almost had to catch my breath, but without a pause or reaction, Joan looked at Faith and said, "What does your gut tell you?"

There were no words for several minutes. I finished cleaning up the blocks and started walking toward the doorway when she asked the question again, "Am I dying?"

As I glanced back at both of them, I saw Joan pull that precious little girl up on the changing table. Without hesitation, their eyes met as she simply replied, "Yes, you are dying."

"I'm not scared," the little voice said. "Are you?"

"No, I'm not scared either," Joan emphatically stated at she brushed the blonde curls away from Faith's face.

Quietly exiting the room, I closed the door behind me. Leaning up against the wall, I took really deep breaths and prayed the tears and emotion I felt would not be visible to her parents. I could not comprehend what I had just seen or heard.

The bravery of that young child and Joan's honesty reminded me that death does not discriminate. I had witnessed a little girl listening to her inner voice and needing confirmation about what her gut was telling her. I wiped away a tear and heard laughter exploding again behind the door. It was the kind of contagious laughter that made me giggle too. As that little giggle came out of my body, the heaviness of the situation did too.

"Her laugh gets to everyone who hears it," a man said as he walked toward me in the hall.

"What a laugh," I replied.

"I'm Jamie, Faith's father," he said.

"You're a lucky man," I replied.

"Yep," he said with a grin. "Without a doubt."

****

Several years later, in 2007, I was given the task of growing the length of stay within our hospice organization. Length of stay is the length of time that a patient remains in hospice care. The median length of stay for a hospice patient is only 23 days out of a 180 day benefit provided by Medicare. The longer individuals recieve hospice care, the better their symptoms are managed and the better prepared their families are to deal with death. Additionally, longer lengths of stay on hospice are associated with an increased trust and stronger relationship with the patient's clincial care team (composed of a hospice team, primary care physician, and also any specialty physicians the patient requires.)

Hospice care is typically reimbursed on a per diem rate that Medicare offers, so the organization must apply that rate to the length of a patient's stay, regardless of how long or short. Hospice care is usually more expensive for the hospice organization when patients are first admitted due to pain management, initial visits by hospice staff for assessment, and the provision of any medical equipment and prescriptions that the patient requires. Hospice care is also more expensive for the hospice organization towards the end of a patient's life while maintaining comfort and family support. The longer a patient receives hospice care, the longer the hospice orgnization is able to stretch the costs of patient care to provide a break even bottomline.

In my experience, there was constant chatter in leadeship meetings to bring more patients onto our hospice program for longer periods. At times, the pressure for earlier referrals and larger volumes of admitted patients seemed to blur the focus of the organization's intentions. I pondered and fought internally while maintaining the focus on the true mission of hospice, which is to serve people wherever they are in their disease process (whether they were diagnosed with a terminal illness early or later in their prognosis).

There were several moments throughout my career that I witnessed the grassroots movement begin to evaporate that Dame Cicely Saunders had envisioned and intended for hospice. Hospice was becoming part of the medical model of care in the United States, which was positive. But a trend of increased regulations and restrictions began to negatively impact delivery of care to people with chronic illness.

In addition, the battle with local physicians prolonging suffering as they continued to provide expensive, extensive and agressive treatment for dying patients had become epic. In a fee for service medical culture, the more treatment given, the more reimbursement the physician receives. I started to question the intention of our healthcare system that seemed focused on profit instead of focused on inclusion and patient-centered care. As a hospice organization, we were conforming to our environment instead of offering a "solution" to the existing healthcare culture, which is what Dame Cicely Saunders intended for the hospice care movement.

Proudly, at the end of the day, I worked for a hospice orgization that successfully maintained a balance of being fiscally sound enough to provide services for many years in the future for our community without ever compromising the delivery of excellant care at the bedside.

Even with the constant changing of healthcare culture, I still had a job to do. I was charged with increasing patient population and length of stay. How was I going to creatively approach my assignment? How would I create a campaign that was received positively by the community and still fulfill the goals put before my team to increase the number of patients being referred? It was a challenge to my mind, body, and spirit.

In the midst of it all, I recalled the conversation between Faith and our hospice nurse in that beautiful, emerald green eyed, blonde haired little girl's room. I remembered Joan asking her, "What does your gut say?"

I began to ask myself that very question. "What does my gut say?" It told me to make sure I didn't try to convince people but instead empower them, to make end of life choices that were right for them. It told me to encourage choice, even if it meant choosing not to have hospice care.

I rounded up my entire marketing staff along with a few high-level clinicians and began the conversation about how we would address the community. It was an opportunity for us to grow as an in-house agency, but also for me to grow as a person. We as a team were on a mission to challenge our community and inspire people to make decisions about their own end of life choices.

As I researched programs already developed in other markets that might be a good fit for our area, I could only recall Bud Hammes' "Respecting Choices" campaign. I had spoken with him one time before and was amazed at the progress his organization had made to engage his community in conversations about death and dying. He completely blew me away with his success. Of the people in La Crosse, WI., 93 percent had advance care planning on file at the local hospital.

Dreaming big, I wanted to emulate or at least duplicate his success in my service area. Working from his campaign model, we brainstormed and came up with a plan. I wanted color, a mascot, and evidence-based materials that would empower our community. I wanted to inspire and encourage individuals to reclaim death from our healthcare system and to start talking about life and end of life choices and desires.

What would we name it? "How about 'Start the Conversation,'" one team member offered. The consensus was that name suggested that the conversation could end.

"How about 'Begin the Conversation?'" another one chimed in. That was it. I remember running up the back stairs and Googling the domain name. I immediately purchased BeginTheConversation.org for $9.99.

In April of 2008, we began developing the campaign to address advance care planning across our five-county area. My gut was telling me a few things. Make it a separate website without a connection to our hospice organization. Make it colorful and lighthearted. Appeal to 40-year olds and above.

I worked with Hillary Hoggard, an experienced graphic designer who had worked on the set of "Lord of the Rings" in New Zealand. The campaign took months to finalize with input from board members and my marketing staff. During that time, we decided to include the regional medical community in the campaign focus. We knew that healthcare employees in general were good about sharing what should be done but not so good at implementing their own advice, so we chose to reach out to them as we incorporated a marketing plan to include the medical industry in addition to the community at large.

By August, just two months prior to launching the "Begin the Conversation" campaign, we were excited about the message and the opportunity to educate both the community and healthcare workers about a new way to talk about death. We were in the final stages of design when two things happened, the Grammy Awards aired on television and I heard a story about a local 18-year old freshman who was attending the University of North Carolina Wilmington (UNCW).

I was surprised at how much those two factors affected the outcome of the campaign. Both influences were major game changers.

I remember sitting in my living room as the awards show aired in the background. I didn't pay much attention until some guy ripped a Grammy right out of Taylor Swift's hand. I looked up to see him grabbing the microphone as he raged on about why his friend should have won the award. As the network quickly cut to commercial, I thought to myself, "What just happened?"

Later in the ceremony, a beautiful African-American woman came up to accept her award. It was the same woman the man on stage had been referring to earlier as he verbally attacked Taylor Swift. As I watched everything unfold, I was shocked at how the celebrity thanked everyone, then unselfishly invited Swift to join her on stage to share her moment. It was Beyoncé, and I immediately wanted to know her. As I purchased her album online, I thought to myself, "I have to support those willing to do the right thing at the right time."

It was at that moment I knew "Begin the Conversation" needed to be affiliated with our hospice organization after all. The community needed to know who was trying to do the right thing. They needed to know who was investing their efforts into the community and the healthcare industry to begin conversations that were relevant to end of life.

Three weeks later, I sat once again on my living room floor working on the campaign that was a mere 34 days from its launch. As the local news blared in the background, something grabbed my attention for a second time. A woman was crying and thanking the community for all their love and support. She was mourning the loss of her son who had been tragically killed by a lightning strike while surfing near Johnny Mercer's Pier in Wrightsville Beach, N.C. Her son had just arrived from Raleigh to attend UNCW. His life was taken instantly, and the mother's words, "I wish I had known if he wanted to be buried or cremated," haunted me.

The Grammy Awards and the death of that young student drastically changed my direction for the campaign. My gut told me to expand our target audience to reach a younger generation. I thought about it for a long time. Young drivers make end of life choices when they choose to be organ donors, so why not expand the campaign demographics to include 18-year-olds so they can learn about other end of life options?

After the Labor Day holiday, I met with the CEO at hospice and pitched the completed "Begin the Conversation" campaign. My gut told me this would be the greatest, most creative accomplishment of my hospice career. I presented a movement to my boss that epitomized my team's concepts through design, layout, and language that reached people in our intended demographic. I even included a mascot, an elephant, known as "the elephant in the room." Within moments of the presentation, both me and the elephant were completely deflated.

"What about the politics of it all?" were the first words out of my boss' mouth.

I thought about two nasty words a colleague of mine had said five months into the campaign development. "Death panels." Speechless, yet ignited at the same time, I said with enthusiasm, "It may not be great timing, but people are talking about death and dying."

"This could be considered a risky campaign right now," my boss said, confused by my excitement.

"I know," I said with confidence. "But we must be part of the conversation. If we call ourselves experts at end of life care, we have to stand up and empower individuals to reclaim death from the medical community. No one should tell us how to die. Not a doctor or nurse, not our parents and especially not our government. Death and dying will always be on the edge of controversy."

Without saying another word, my boss glanced over my presentation materials, looked back at the unpublished website on her screen, and nodded her head. She gave me the green light to "Begin the Conversation."

As I left her office, I turned to her and said one last thing. "Part of the campaign is to implement a Facebook page."

"What is Facebook?" She asked.

****

I learned early in my career to listen to my gut from a very conscious five-year old facing her own end of life. I have thought about Faith many times. When my inner voice starts to speak, I hear Faith's explosive laughter deep in my heart.

It was that contagious laughter that empowered me to trust my gut, put my faith in a napkin note, and walk away from a 17-year career in hospice. The industry was changing, and I knew deep down in my gut that I wasn't changing with it. It was time to take a leap of faith and leave the familiar. It was time to move beyond titles and salaries and lean into the unknown.

It was time for me to begin putting the life lessons learned into practice. It was time to tell a different story. It was time to introduce the world to the greatest teachers in my life that taught me about life. It was just time.

"Sometimes you have to die a little inside
in order to be reborn and rise again as
a stronger and wiser version of you." -Unknown

122

CHAPTER FOURTEEN
Life Lesson: Closure is just a myth.

"Let the world unfold without always attempting to figure it all out."
—*Wayne Dyer*

I recall talking with Dr. Dawn Gross during a recording of a Death by Design podcast during season one. She suddenly stated, "Closure is a myth. When you love, journey with individuals, and treat patients who die, there is no such thing as closure. You carry all the individuals that have died with you throughout your life."

It was in those moments that I realized the grief of loss would never leave me, and that I would have to learn to carry it each day. Some individuals say, "The grief you feel is a testimony of the love you gave and received." I'm not sure how I feel about that statement. All I know is that I would never trade the love, the laughter, and the life lessons in exchange for the grief I carry for those I've lost over the years.

When I get really still and quiet, I realize it's my responsibility to keep living each day to the fullest because of all those I've lost. I can't get weighted down. I must carry forward knowing that my life is richer because of the experiences I've encountered with those who have faced end of life.

****

What is grief to you?

For me, grief is like a backpack filled with 200 pounds of large rocks.

My backpack is very heavy to carry. Knowing that I can never put my backpack down, it has permanently saddened and disheartened me. My backpack has become part of my shadow. Some days, I can't shoulder the weight. It is hard to even function, and many times I can't recall my life without my backpack.

Over time, the load seems to feel lighter, but I still carry the same 200 pounds of rock. With each passing day, my body adjusts. I become stronger and my heart begins to feel again. It may be a week, a month or many years before the heaviness of the load in my backpack is lifted.

Carrying my backpack has forced me into a rebirth of sorts; a rebirth to a different and unrecognizable life that leads to moving beyond something ... or someone. Like giving birth, I am laboring through the heavy, dark weight of my backpack to hear the cry of life once more.

For me, grief is a backpack full of heavy rocks that can never be put down. But I am learning to carry my backpack everyday throughout my life.

So, I ask again ... What is grief to you?

"Never stop learning, because
life never stops teaching." —Unknown

CHAPTER FIFTEEN

Life Lesson: Be authentic ... Just be.

"Be authentic. Be genuine. Be real. Be yourself." —Tai Sheridan

Throughout my years in hospice care, as I've grown older, I've learned that being authentic is one of the greatest gifts you can give yourself and others. Throughout life we conform to rules, peer pressure, and other elements of life to fit in and to feel valued and worthy of love.

In conclusion, after living, writing and reading these stories within Bridging The Gap, I noticed one common thread of similarity reflected within each of these experiences. They're authentic, they're real and it took vulnerability to share them with a stanger.

Each of these individuals within these stories didn't need my acceptance, my approval or my love, nor were they looking for it. I just happened to cross their path, pause, listen and allowed their humanness to impact my life. In the spirit of this common thread, I thought the best way to conclude my journey with you would be to share my story in the most authentic way I know how by including it within these pages.

****

Growing up, my dad always reminded me that time passes by so fast. He often reiterated there was no need to rush tomorrow because the day was not over yet. His advice stayed with me through the years, but there were many times in my adolescence that all I could focus on was the next day, so I could start living life on my own.

I was a lazy, bored high school student who rushed home every day at 1:45 p.m. to watch my stories. Soap operas were an integral part of my day, and I lived vicariously through the characters and story plots of daytime television.

I wanted to be a part of it all. It didn't matter if I was acting, writing, casting or even one of the lowest unpaid interns, I was going to be in the business. I was convinced it was a part of my destiny and embedded in my DNA.

I grew up in a very dark, emotional, almost formidable household during my teen years. There were two factors that kept me connected to my creativity. One was my dream of becoming a part of daytime television. The other was my interaction with the youth group at Winfree Memorial Baptist Church. Without those two influences during my turbulent years, I often wonder who I would be today.

I was the middle child in my family. Born July 12, 1971 at 12:43 p.m., I weighed 7 pounds, 12 ounces. As a young girl, I considered myself intuitive and sensitive. I felt people's emotions and always tried to connect with just about anyone who crossed my path, but not everyone could see that, because I was also an introvert. I never felt I needed people in my life, and even at a young age I carefully chose my friends. I made a handful of lifelong friends along the way who were always easy to reconnect with no matter how long we were separated.

I always envied my older sister and younger brother and felt that they received most of the attention growing up. I believe that my resentment forced me to seek out a substitute to fill a void in my life. Luckily, it was a church family that proved to be a solid foundation for me to build upon and inspired me to follow Christ. I found one simple principle to guide me through my turmoil, and that was love.

Before graduating from high school, I begged and pleaded with my parents that college was not for me. I longed to head to New York or Los Angeles to be close to all things creative. I wanted to embrace different cultures and alternative ways of thinking. I wished for the opportunity to engage with artists and people who were gay, but my parents had other plans for me.

As I sat crying in the stairwell of my childhood home, I realized that my dreams were suddenly crushed. It would be much later before I learned that closed doors and failures would lead me to a life I never expected.

I applied to colleges and was accepted by only a handful. During that time, I knew I had to embrace my second passion … my faith. The day after high school graduation, I found myself on a plane headed for Houston, Texas, to become a sojourner. My assignment was to work with other high school grads and college students on mission work within the United States. I was assigned to Millard McWhorter.

I was scared, but to stay back in Virginia was even scarier. I wanted adventure. I needed space from my dysfunctional family unit that was causing my heart to harden. I realized that the troubled, dark, and unforgiving environment at home was no longer my cross to bear. It was time to move onward and upward.

I lived at the Baptist Center on Gano Street in downtown Houston. The area was known for inner-city Hispanic gangs and large numbers of young children left to provide for themselves throughout the summer.

For three months, I lived with four other college students and learned how to dodge huge water bugs and eat things past their expiration date. I wrote my friends back home describing how I worked and played with the Hispanic children in the neighborhood and taught them about Christ. I shared how I had learned to lead by example just by loving them.

Although I had found peace and comfort within those dark streets of Houston I called home, I needed something more. One evening, sitting on my Gano Street rooftop overlooking the city, I confided in my friend, Traci, and decided to give college a try. She was headed to Meredith College back in Raleigh, N.C., to finish her senior year, and I followed suit.

Throughout my days at Meredith, I gathered wisdom from the mistakes I made. I dated a lot of wrong people but made lifelong friends at the same time. The creative person deep inside my soul, however, was still there longing for adventure.

Right after I graduated from college, I attended a family reunion on Topsail Island in North Carolina that totally redirected my path. My second cousin, Teresa, who lived in Brooklyn, convinced me to follow my gut, move to New York City and give it at least a year.

With one hundred dollars in my pocket, I packed my Honda Accord and drove to New York City. I was confident that I had taken the traditional path expected of me and accomplished my parents' goals. My life had suddenly become mine. It was my adventure, and I was determined to follow the dreams of the 14-year old girl still living inside me. My long-awaited journey to New York had finally begun, and the city was my playground.

When I arrived at Teresa's brownstone in Brooklyn, I quickly realized that I would be sharing a room with a two-year old. I learned that vodka and orange juice, known as a screwdriver, was not my friend. In fact, after that first night in NYC, I've never be able to drink one again. After a few days, I started to devise a plan. Teresa made a list of all her connections in the television industry and called in favors to get me as many interviews as she possibly could.

One of her friends, Judy, worked on the set of "Another World" and gave me an interview. The production studio was in Brooklyn, but her office was in Rockefeller Center. I spent the entire day educating myself on the subway and bus system of New York. I was also challenged by how to walk through the revolving doors of one the greatest networks in the broadcast industry, NBC.

I walked through security that blocked all entrances to the production floors high above the streets and took the elevator to level five to wait for Judy to see me. Sitting in the small reception area, I noticed many familiar faces breeze in and out of the office. They were all faces I knew from television. I felt like I was in the twilight zone.

"Mrs. Miller will see you now," a voice said, suddenly interrupting my thoughts. I stood up and followed the receptionist down a small corridor.

"Mrs. Miller," she said. "Kim Paul is here to see you."

Mrs. Miller stood up and greeted me. After I explained how I was related to Teresa and outlined my goals as professionally as I knew how, she sat behind her desk and looked at me with a hint of pity in her eyes.

"I don't have anything right now," she said. "But let me call upstairs."

Three weeks later I was hired by "Saturday Night Live," where I worked in studio 8H on the set of the live broadcast at 11:30pm. I worked there for over a year until I was offered a higher paying job at CBS as a casting assistant for daytime television.

My dream had become a reality, but I was unhappy and lost. Something was missing. I often looked outside my CBS office window and watched millions of people rush to their destinations. I felt like I was looking down from a verrada at a sea of people living their true lives and the view made me question my own aspirations; was I living a life that was true to me? My life long dream was over. Now what?

All I wanted to do was go home. I wanted to get in my car and drive until I was free of the sky scrapper walls that had deceived me. After two weeks notice, I left CBS. I packed my car and headed toward Garner, N.C.

As I drove south, I thought to myself, "You got exactly what you asked for, but you didn't want it." My dream of working in television was over. I wanted nothing more to do with the entertainment business, so I walked away.

By 1998, I was settled back into familiar territory with some of my college friends from Meredith who were still around, and I worked three jobs. I worked full-time for a local non-profit, Resource For Seniors. I woke up at 3:30 a.m. to unload UPS cargo planes and even umpired junior league baseball games on the weekend. I found happiness in connecting with people once again.

I started writing and journaling. I thought about applying to the FBI. I started training, joined the Navy Reserves' Intel unit, and then quickly realized I had no business taking a government job.

I met a boy, and he broke my heart. My creative side awakened once again. I moved to the East Coast Hollywood hoping for another shot at a production position.

Some might say that I have lived many lives within the one I was given. I would agree.

Making the decision to move to Wilmington, near a growing film industry, was a way to endure loss, but it led me to exactly where I was supposed to be. At times, I'm even shocked, but I've always trusted that everything happens for a reason and that life is a true mystery. Only when I stopped trying to figure life out and leaned into the mystery did I start to see small and big miracles happen in my life every day. There were many times that I received job offers from Los Angeles and local productions, but I was learning something more important. I was learning about life through individuals who had lived it and were dying.

These lessons changed me, opened my eyes to what really matters, and taught me to embrace the unknown, because if you are quiet and still long enough, your life might just find you. I believe my life found me without much effort from little ole imperfect me.

Most individuals who see "Saturday Night Live," CBS daytime casting, or my film involvement on my resumé often ask tons of questions about my experiences. I assure them that the greatest experience for me has been telling real life stories and learning life lessons from people I barely knew. I am thankful I was present long enough to realize the gifts I was given and apply the lessons I've learned to the rest of my life.

These life lessons are from those who have graced my life. Each lesson has been tattooed on my heart. My hope is that you will see the lessons and that your heart will be open to accept the gifts they brought to me. I hope you can personally connect with these stories that inspired me to live a life designed around what matters most. I hope you are inspired too.

I believe you end up exactly where you are supposed to be no matter how hard you try to avoid the whispers of your life calling you toward your purpose. I truly found mine.

As I begin to pack up my Wilmington home and research RV's, I feel the open road calling me and my side kick, Haven. I remember the life lessons each of these stories have taught me. It is time to share the lessons, travel, and continue to learn about life. This past year has been a dream come true. Writing this book, recording Death by Design podcasts, meeting kindred spirits via phone, Skype, and in person have all taught me to say yes to living.

Thanks, Miss Norma. Thanks to your legacy, I'm going to *Hit The Road* too.

Haven and I will be traveling over the next year, hopefully visiting all continental states. I can't wait to share our journey on the road with you and those in hospice care, as we all face each day as if it were our last.

Thank you for reading this book. I hope to meet each of you somewhere along the road. You can follow us at www.deathbydesign.com.

Remember that your voice does matter. The way you live your life can change another life. When it comes right down to it, what matters most is love. And it all begins with loving yourself.

ACKNOWLEDGEMENTS

"Some people come in your life as blessings.
Some come in your life as lessons." — *Mother Teresa*

To Apple, to Frank, to little Faith, Miss Norma, and the many other individuals that crossed my path over the past 18 years while working in end of life —

I never thought I would leave my career in hospice, but each of you inspired me to implement the life lessons you taught me throughout the years. After taking a year off to write this book, I hear the faint whisper of a distant call. I think it is my life calling me, asking me to travel, to tell your stories in hopes that they will inspire more individuals to build a life around what matters most. Maybe your stories will change how others live and die beyond just me. Maybe together we will be forever a part of each other's legacy.

You made me realize you can't change people; you just have to love them and accept them, and look deep within for the lesson being taught. At times, you find others teaching you, and at times you find yourself as the teacher. In hindsight, after writing your stories, I have realized the full effect that each of you has had on my life. I'm not sure why you chose me, but you are forever scored on my heart.

I still carry the stories you shared and the lives you lived with me. I see each of your faces, hear each of your voices, and feel your presence, and as promised, I have kept some parts of our stories solely between us.

Thank you for being vulnerable, for sharing your life stories with me, and for revealing moments of your life with me. Thank you for trusting me to tell these life lessons so others will know you and celebrate the wisdom you bestowed on me.

You've made me believe that there are no coincidences and that everything happens for a reason, even if I don't quite understand. You each taught me to live on the edge and live boldly. You taught me not to settle for the ordinary, but to see the extraordinary in every moment of life. You taught me to believe in something greater than myself. You taught me love, forgiveness, and humor.

I will not waste this rare opportunity to embrace life and even death on my own terms.

I promise to think of each of you often, and I promise not to be sad but instead to remember the laughter, the advice, the vulnerability, the kindness, the rare moments, and the many life lessons you taught me. I promise to live, knowing each of you are walking beside me every step of the way.

Love,

Kimberly

DISCUSSIONS QUESTIONS

Life Lesson 1: Miracles Happen Every Day

Have you noticed small miracles on a normal day of living? If so, what were they?

Do you believe miracles happen every day?

Define miracles.

Describe a miracle that you observed.

What did you feel while reading this chapter?

Life Lesson 2: Connection is the reason we are alive

Have you communicated to your family about your end of life wishes?

Why do you think it is so hard to communicate about these hard subjects?

Have you completed your Advance Care Planning?

Where is it located?

Have you communicated with your healthcare power of attorney?

Life Lesson 3: It is the Simple Things that Matter The Most

What simple things matter to you in life ?

Why do you think simple things matter most?

What would be on your bucket list if you were facing a serious illness?

Make a list of things that you hope to accomplish in the next 12 months.

Life Lesson 4: Death Will Come To Us All

What was the first thing you thought about on September 11, 2001?

Who did you think about during that moment?

Did you reach out and call someone you loved?

What did you realize about life after September 11, 2001?

Life Lesson 5: Advocate For others

Have you ever had the opportunity to advocate for someone you loved?

How did it make you feel?

Did you feel prepared to advocate on behalf of your loved one?

Are you someone's healthcare power of attorney, proxy, or chosen one to speak on behalf of a loved one if they cannot communicate?

How does being selected for that role make you feel?

Life Lesson 6: Forgiveness

Have you ever forgiven someone?

What feelings were brought up within you when you read this chapter?

Have you ever been forgiven?

Why do you think people do not forgive others?

Who do you think suffers when forgiveness is not offered?

Life Lesson 7: Unconditional Love

Have you felt unconditional love?

What does unconditional love mean to you?

Who do you love unconditionally?

Make a list of individuals you want to call, write a note to, and express how much they mean to you.

Life Lesson 8: Ask For What You Want

Looking back on your life, do you recall a situation in which you wish you'd asked for something, but didn't?

Have you asked for something you wanted?

Why didn't you ask for what you wanted?

Make a list of things you would like and make a timeline to ask.

Life Lesson 9: Wisdom Trumps Education

Have you ever felt you were projecting the death you wanted for someone onto them?

Have you witnessed others projecting the death they want for the individual onto them?

How do you separate your desires versus what a loved one or friend desires at their end of life?

Do you think it is a gift to be informed about what individuals want if they become seriously ill or sick?

Life Lesson 10: Life is a Mystery

Have you ever experienced anything in life that can't be explained?

Do you believe that spiritual communication can happen with loved ones that have passed?

Do you dream about loved ones that are no longer living?

Life Lesson 11: Change your Perspective, Change your Life

Have you changed your opinion about something when you changed your perspective?

Are you sensitive to other individuals' perspectives?

Have you ever experienced a paradigm shift?

Life Lesson 12: Physicians are not God, They're Just Human

Have you ever experienced a mistake made by a physician or the healthcare system?

If so, how did you handle it?

How does your opinion of physicians vary from what your parents thought?

Do you believe individuals working in healthcare are doing the best that they can?

How would you like to see healthcare change to enhance better end of life care?

Life Lesson 13: Trust Your Gut

Do you believe in gut feelings?

Have you every trusted your gut to make a big decision?

When was the last time you trusted your gut to make a decision?

Have you ever regretted not trusting your gut?

Life Lesson 14: Closure is a Myth

Have you lost someone close to you? Who was it?

Do you believe in closure when someone close to you dies?

Have you ever felt grief?

How did you handle your grief?

Life Lesson 15: If you are Still Long Enough, Your Life will Find You

Do you think everything happens for a reason?

Have you found your life, or has your life found you?

How do you make major changes in your life?

GLOSSARY

Advance Care Planning (ACP): An ongoing process of conversations between you, your family, and loved ones, and your healthcare providers that includes the communication and documentation of your values, beliefs, and wishes for future healthcare treatments. ACP includes all types of care you would or would not want to receive if you are unable to communicate your choices.

Advance Directive: A legal document that states the medical treatments and/or life-sustaining measures you would or would not want should an end-of-life situation occur and render you unable to communicate your choices. It is your written healthcare plan.

Advance Instruction for Mental Health: A legal document that tells healthcare providers what types of mental health treatments you want and don't want. Your mental health instructions can be included in this separate document or combined with a Healthcare Power of Attorney or General Power of Attorney.

Antibiotics: Medications used to fight infections.

Anatomical Study: A person may allow his/her body to be studied after death by scientists and other healthcare-related researchers to gain knowledge about certain diseases and the dying process. This may eventually lead to improved care of others living with similar conditions.

Artificial Nutrition Hydration (Fluids): When you are unable to eat or drink on your own, nutrition and hydration can be administered into your stomach through a feeding tube.

Autopsy: An examination of your body after your death to determine the cause of death or the extent of changes produced by a disease.

Begin The Conversation: An advance care planning program created to encourage the use of advance care directives, was created in 2009 by Wilmington, North Carolina-based Lower Cape Fear Hospice. Designed to help everyone prepare for the unexpected, the goal is to encourage everyone to complete advance care directives with a focus on the value of conversations in advance care planning.

Cardio-Pulmonary Resuscitation (CPR): When your heart and/or breathing stops, CPR can be used to start them again. It can be done through mouth-to-mouth resuscitation, chest compressions, or defibrillator machines.

Census: An official count or survey of a population, typically recording various details of individuals. Hospice Census: individuals who are recieving hospice care at a given moment.

Chronic Illness: A human health condition or disease that is persistent or otherwise long-lasting in its effects, or a disease that comes with time. The term chronic is usually applied when the course of the disease lasts for more than three months. Common chronic diseases include arthritis, asthma, cancer, COPD, diabetes and viral diseases such as hepatitis C and HIV/AIDS.

Cremation: The disposal of a dead person's body by burning it to ashes, typically before a funeral ceremony.

Decision-Making Ability (Capacity): The ability to make decisions. A person has the ability and right to make his/her own healthcare decisions unless it is shown he/she cannot understand, communicate, or process information needed to make those decisions.

Death by Design Podcast: An educational podcast that creates a community for artists, clinicians, photographers, podcasters, and individuals personal experiences about end of life.

Dame Cecily Saunders: (22 June 1918 – 14 July 2005) An English Anglican nurse, social worker, physician, and writer involved with many international universities. She is best known for her role in the birth of the hospice movement, emphasising the importance of palliative care in modern medicine.

Design Thinking: Creative strategies that designers use during the process of designing. Design thinking is also an approach that can be used to consider issues, with a means to help resolve these issues, more broadly than within professional design practice and has been applied in business as well as social issues. Design thinking in business uses the designer's sensibility and methods to match people's needs with what is technologically feasible and what a viable business strategy can convert into customer value and market opportunity.

Designing Your End of Life: A method of applying design thinking to create your end of life wishes in Advance Care Planning documents, communicating that to loved ones, and making it digital, or written, for easy access.

Disposition of Remains: A few options exist for the final placement of your body after death that include burial and cremation. Having conversations with loved ones about these options before death can help alleviate possible conflict.

Do Not Resuscitate Order (DNR): A medical order obtained through your physician, the DNR indicates you do not want to receive resuscitation attempted if your heart or breathing stops.

Electroconvulsive Treatment (ECT): A procedure in which electric currents are passed through the brain. These currents can cause changes in the brain that can reverse symptoms of certain types of mental illness when other treatments do not work.

Feeding Tube: A flexible tube that is inserted through the pharynx and into the stomach through which liquid food is passed. Feeding tubes provide nutrition for those who cannot obtain it by mouth, are unable to swallow safely, or need supplemental nutrition.

Green Burial: A burial designed to have minimal environmental impact, typically with a corpse that has not been embalmed being placed in a biodegradable coffin or bag and buried in a grave marked with a sapling.

Guardian: A person who is appointed to act on your behalf if you are unable to make your own decisions and there are no other people who are able or available.

Healthcare Power of Attorney (Document): A legal document you prepare that names another person to be your healthcare decision-maker when you are unable to communicate your own choices.

HIPAA Release Form: A legal document that authorizes the release of your protected healthcare information to a specified person. It can include all healthcare information or can stipulate that certain details be excluded.

Hospice Care: Hospice provides healthcare services and support for those living with advance illness and focuses on pain relief and symptom management, patient and family assistance, and end-of-life education and support.

Hospice Care Medicare Benefit: Hospice is paid for through the Medicare Hospice Benefit, Medicaid Hospice Benefit, and most private insurers. If a person does not have coverage through Medicare, Medicaid, or a private insurance company, hospice will work with the person and their family to ensure needed services can be provided.

IV Fluids: Liquids, such as medicine, blood, or nutrients, that are administered directly into a vein.

Intubation: Intubation is the passage of a tube through your mouth into your lungs. Ventilation is when air is passed through that tube to allow you to breath.

Length of Stay (LOS): A term to describe the duration of a single episode of hospitalization or the days within hospice care. Inpatient days are calculated by subtracting day of admission from day of discharge.

Life Support/Life-Sustaining Treatments: These are medical procedures that maintain your bodily functions (i.e. breathing, heart-beating) when you are incapable of doing them independently. They can include procedures such as ventilation, dialysis, surgery, transfusions, antibiotics, and artificial nutrition and hydration.

Living Will (Document): A legal document that expresses your choices related to future healthcare treatments and life-sustaining measures at end of life.

Innovation: Viewed as the application of better solutions that meet new requirements, unarticulated needs, or existing market needs. This is accomplished through more effective products, processes, services, technologies, or business models that are readily available to markets, governments, and society. The term "innovation" can be defined as something original and more effective and, as a consequence, new, that "breaks into" the market or society.

National Healthcare Decision Day (NHDD): Exists to inspire, educate, and empower the public and providers about the importance of advance care planning. NHDD is an initiative to encourage patients to express their wishes regarding healthcare and for providers and facilities to respect those wishes, whatever they may be. Normally recognized on April 16th every year.

Natural Death: A natural death occurs when you decide to not have treatments or measures to delay the moment of death. It applies only when death is near and will happen from natural causes.

Medical Aid In Dying: Medical aid in dying (sometimes called death with dignity) is a safe and trusted medical practice. It allows a terminally ill, mentally capable adult who has a prognosis of six months or less to live to request and obtain from her or his doctor, and self-ingest — if suffering becomes unbearable — medication that brings about a peaceful death. This is the accurate description of the practice, and its words signal the strict eligibility criteria and key safeguards.

MOST/POLST: A national movement, the POLST (Physicians Orders for Life Sustaining Measures) was started to improve quality of healthcare by translating people's choices into medical orders. It is the basis for the MOST documents (Medical Orders for Scope of Treatment) and includes communication between you, your decision-making agents, and your healthcare providers.

Organ, Eye, and Tissue Donation: To donate organs, eyes, or tissue to another person in medical need, you should document your wishes and communicate them to loved ones.

Palliative Care: Medical care to relieve pain, discomfort, or distress. It does not include curative treatments or life-sustaining measures, nor does it include any measures meant to hasten or expedite death. Palliative care can be provided at any time during your illness to alleviate symptoms or pain.

Preplanning Funeral Arrangements: To pre-pay for your funeral expenses prior to your death including burial, obituary, and all expenses related to the burial costs.

Referrals: An act of referring someone or something for consultation, review, or further action, the directing of a patient to a medical specialist by a primary care physician, a person whose case has been referred to a specialist doctor or a professional body (Hospice and Palliative Care).

Revoke/Revocation: To put an end to or discontinue an advance care planning document. Revocation processes can include destroying the forms or creating a new form. If you do revoke an ACP document, it should be communicated to your healthcare agents and providers.

Serious Illness: A program facilitates appropriate conversations between clinicians, seriously ill patients, and their families. Drawn from best practices in palliative care, the intervention provides guidance for clinicians to initiate these difficult conversations in the right way, at the right time.

Surrogate/ Proxy: A person with the ability and authority to make healthcare-related decisions on your behalf. This person could be your next of kin, an appointed representative, or your Healthcare Power of Attorney (if the form is in place).

Terry Schavio: The Terri Schiavo case was a right-to-die legal case in the United States from 1990 to 2005, involving Theresa Marie "Terri" Schiavo (December 3, 1963 – March 31, 2005), a woman in an irreversible persistent vegetative state. Schiavo's husband and legal guardian argued that Schiavo would not have wanted prolonged artificial life support without the prospect of recovery, and he elected to remove her feeding tube. Schiavo's parents disputed her husband's assertions and challenged Schiavo's medical diagnosis, arguing in favor of continuing artificial nutrition and hydration. The highly publicized and prolonged series of legal challenges presented by her parents, which ultimately involved state and federal politicians up to the level of President George W. Bush, caused a seven-year delay before Schiavo's feeding tube was ultimately removed.

Traditional Burial: To describe a "traditional burial" is a bit difficult. Burials today can be as varied as the personalities of the deceased. Some people are buried at sea; some, today, are buried "naturally" – in other words without the use of a casket – and still others are never buried at all.

Volunteer Stop Eating and Drinking (VSED): VSED stands for voluntarily stopping eating and drinking—an intentional decision to stop drinking liquids and eating food—for the specific purpose of causing death. It does not refer to stopping food and fluids provided by means of a feeding tube or to situations in which a patient has no appetite or is unable to eat or drink due to illness or disease. Death takes place within 5 to 21 days. The cause of death is dehydration.

RESEARCH

Abba K, Byrne P, Horton S, Lloyd-Williams M (2013). Interventions to Encourage Discussion of End-of-Life Preferences Between Members of the General Population and the People Closest to Them - A Systematic Review. BMC Palliative Care, 12, 40. www.biomedcentral.com/1472-684X/12/40

Alano GJ, Pekmezaris R, Tai JY, Hussain MJ, Jeune J, Louis B, El-Kass G, Ashraf MS, Reddy R, Lesser M, Wolf-Klein GP (2010).Factors Influencing Older Adults to Complete Advance Directives. Palliative and Supportive Care, 8(3): 267-275.

American Bar Association (n.d.). Law for Older Adults. Health Care Directives: What is the Patient Self-Determination Act? www.americanbar.org/groups/public_education/resources/law_issues_for_consumers/patient_self_determination_act.html

Ariés P (1981). The Hour of Our Death: The Classic History of Western Attitudes Toward Death Over the Last One Thousand Years.(2nd Vintage Books, Kindle ed.). (Weaver, H., Trans.) New York, NY: Vintage Books.

Benson WF, Aldrich N (2012). Advance Care Planning: Ensuring Your Wishes Are Known and Honored If You Are Unable to Speak forYourself. Retrieved from CDC: www.cdc.gov/aging/pdf/advanced-care-planning-critical-issue-brief.pdf

Bloche M. Gregg (2005). Managing Conflict at the End of Life. New England Journal of Medicine. 352 (23): 2371-2373.www.nejm.org/doi/full/10.1056/NEJMp058104

Bowron C (2012, February 17). Our Unrealistic Attitudes About Death, Through a Doctor's Eyes. www.washingtonpost.com/opinions/our-unrealistic-views-of-death-through-a-doctors-eyes/2012/01/31/gIQAeaHpJR_story.html

Byoc I (2004). The Four Things that Matter Most: A Book about Living. New York, NY: Free Press.

Emanuel EJ, Emanuel LL (1998). The Promise of a Good Death. The Lancet , 351 (suppl II): 21-29. www.thelancet.com/pdfs/journals/lancet/PIIS0140673698903294.pdf

Fried TR, Redding CA, Robbins ML, O'Leary JR, Iannone L. (2011). Agreement Between Older Persons and Their Surrogate Decision-Makers Regarding Participation in Advance Care Planning. Journal of the American Geriatric Society, 59 (6): 1105-1109.
www.ncbi.nlm.nih.gov/pmc/articles/PMC4036693/

Goold SS, Williams B, Arnold RM (2000). Conflicts Regarding Decisions to Limit Treatment: A Differential Diagnosis. JAMA 283 (7): 909-914. www.jama.jamanetwork.com/article.aspx?articleid=192406

Greco PJ, Schulman KA, Lavizzo-Mourey R, Hansen-Flaschen J (1991). The Patient Self-Determination Act and the Future of Advance Directives. Annals of Internal Medicine , 115 (8): 639-643. www.ncbi.nlm.nih.gov/pubmed/21649619

Johnson N, Cook D, Giacomini M, Willms D (2000). Toward a "Good" Death: End-of-Life Narrative Constructed in an Intensive Care Unit. Culture, Medicine and Psychiatry. 24:275-295. www.link.springer.com/article/10.1023%2FA%3A1005690501494#page-1

Kübler-Ross E (1969). On Death and Dying. New York, NY: Scribner. 40

Leahman D (2004). Why the Patient Self-Determination Act Has Failed. NC Med J, 65 (4): 249-251. www.ncmedicaljournal.com/wp-content/uploads/NCMJ/jul-aug-04/Leahman.pdf

Moskop JC (2004). Improving Care at the End of life: How Advance Care Planning Can Help. Palliative and Supportive Care, 2, 191-197. www.journals.cambridge.org/action/displayAbstract?fromPage=online&aid=289107&fileId=S1478951504040258

Nelson DV, Brown K (2008). AARP Bulletin Poll Getting Ready to Go: Executive Summary, January 2008. www.assets.aarp.org/rgcenter/il/getting_ready.pdf

New Survey Reveals 'Conversation Disconnect.' The Conversation Project. Press Release, September 18, 2013. www.theconversationproject. org/wp-content/uploads/2013/09/TCP-Survey-Release_FINAL-9-18-13.pdf
Niemira D, Townsend T (2009). Chapter 11: Ethics Conflicts in Rural Communities: End-of-Life Decision-

Making. In W. A. Nelson (Ed.), Handbook for Rural Health Care Ethics: A Practical Guide for Professionals (pp. 209-230).Lebanon, NH: Dartmouth College Press. www.geiselmed.dartmouth.edu/cfm/resources/ethics/chapter-11.pdf

Nolan MT, Bruder M (1997). Patients' Attitudes Toward Advance Directives in End-of-Life Treatment Decisions.Nursing Outlook. 1997; 45(5) 204-208. www.ncbi.nlm.nih.gov/pubmed/9364529

Pew 2006: Pew Research Center 2006: Pew Research Center for the People & the Press. Strong Public Support for Right to Die: More Americans Discussing — and Planning — End-of-Life Treatment. Telephone survey of 1,500 older adults conducted Nov. 9-27, 2005 under the direction of Princeton Survey Research Associates International. January 2006. www.people-press.org/report/266/strong-public-support-for-right-to-die

Prepare for Your Care pamphlet. www.prepareforyourcare.org/index.php?info&page=pamphlet

Ramsaroop SD, Reid MC, Adelman RD (2007). Completing an Advance Directive in the Primary Care Setting: What Do We Need for Success? JAGS. 55(2):277-283. www.ncbi.nlm.nih.gov/pubmed/17302667

Robbins M (2011, July 23). Embrace Death, Live Life.www.huffingtonpost.com/mike-robbins/embrace-death-live-life_b_906329.html Smith R (2000). A Good Death. An Important Aim for Health Services and for Us All. BMJ , 320, 129-130.

Steinhauser KE, Clipp EC, McNeilly M, Christakis N A, McIntyre LM, Tulsky JA (2000). In Search of a Good Death: Observations of Patients, Families, and Providers. Ann Intern Med, 132 (10), 825-832. annals.org/article.aspx?articleid=713475 Sudore RL, Fried TR (2010). Redefining the "Planning" in Advance Care Planning: Preparing for End-of-Life Decision Making. Ann Intern Med, 153(4):256-261. www.annals.org/article.aspx?articleid=745978&resultClick=3

Walter T (2003). Historical and Cultural Variants on the Good Death. BMJ, 327, 218.Weaver E, Vaughan T (2013). Successful Intervention: Raising Awareness of Advanced Care Planning (ACP) in the Rural Community Setting. BMJ Supportive & Palliative Care, 3 (2), 233.

Weng K, Lundblad J, Ceronsky L (2009). National Rural Health Association Technical Assistance Project Final Report. Rural Palliative Care Pilot Project. Stratis Health. September 29, 2009. www.stratishealth.org/documents/NRHA_PC_Report_09-09.pdf

Wilkinson A, Wenger N, Shugarman LR, (2007). Literature Review on Advance Directives. www.aspe.hhs.gov/daltcp/reports/2007/advdirlr.htm

KNOWLEDGE IS POWER
Proven facts to motivate action...

• Most Americans (71%) believe it is more important to enhance quality of life for seriously ill patients – even if it means a shorter life – than to extend the life of seriously ill patients through every medical intervention possible. -Regence, 2011

• Only 28% of home healthcare patients, 65% of nursing home residents, and 88% of hospice patients have an advance directive on record.
-Jones, 2011

• Even among severely or terminally ill patients, fewer than 50% had an advance directive in their medical record. -Kass-Bartelmes, 2003

• Senior care professionals surveyed say 70% of family conversations about aging are prompted by an event such as a health crisis or other emergency. -Home Instead Senior Care, U.S. Research Report, 40/70 Rule

• 82% of estate-planning attorneys surveyed recommended having discussion about aging and end-of-life issues before an adult child is 40 and before a parent is 70. -Home Instead Senior Care, U.S. Research Report, 40/70 Rule

• Most people say they prefer to die at home, yet only about one-third of adults have an advance directive expressing their end-of-life care wishes. Among those 60 and older, only about half have completed an advance directive. – Pew, 2006; AARP, 2008

• 34% of American adults are estimated to be conversation avoiders. That means they haven't talked about any important end-of-life issues with their parents or children, or they have only talked about one issue. – Marist Poll

• 66% of family disputes about aging or end-of-life issues that end up in court could have been avoided if a family had clearly discussed and documented wishes in advance. -Home Instead Senior Care, U.S. Research Report, 40/70 Rule

• There's a big gap between what people say they want and what actually happens: 60% say that making sure their family is not burdened by tough decisions is "extremely important," yet 56% have not communicated their end-of-life wishes. -Survey of Californians by the California HealthCare Foundation, 2012

• 70% of people say they prefer to die at home, but 70% die in a hospital, nursing home, or long-term care facility. -Centers for Disease Control, 2005

• 80% of people say if they were seriously ill, they would want to talk to their doctor about end-of-life care, but only 7% report having this important conversation. -California HealthCare Foundation, 2012

• 82% of people say it's important to put their wishes in writing, but only 23% have actually done it. – California HealthCare Foundation, 2012

• 65-76% of doctors whose patients had an advance directive were not aware it existed. – Kass-Bartelmes, 2003

RESOURCES

End of Life Resources

Death by Design – www. deathbydesign.com
Compassion and Choices – www.compassionandchoices.org
The Art of Dying Magazine – www.artofdyingmagazine.com
Let's Talk About Death – www.letstalkaboutdeath.xyz
End of Life University – www.eoluniversity.com
Tim Ihrig & Associates – www.ihrigmd.com
National Hospice & Palliative Care Organization – www.nhpco.org
American Association of Retired Persons (AARP) – www.aarp.org
Alzheimer's Association – alz.org
American Bar Association – www.americanbar.org/aba.html
Caring Connections· www.caringinro.org
Center for Practical Biotethics – www.practicalbioethics.org
Death with Dignity – www.deathwithdignity.org
Donate Life America – www.donatelife.net
National Cancer Institute – www.cancer.gov
National Institute on Aging – www.nia.nih.gov
U.S. Department of Health & Human Services – www.hhs.gov
Living with Serious Illness – www.seriousillness.org
Coalition to Transform Advanced Care – www.thectac.org
The Center for Advance Palliative Care (CAPC) – www.capc.org
The End Well Project – www.endwellproject.com
Ungerleider Palliative Care Education Fund – www.shoshanaungerleider.com
The Carolina Center for Hospice & Palliative Care – www.cchospice.org

Recommended Books

Napkin Notes Dad – Garth Callighan
Extreme Measures – Jessica Zitter
Caring for the Dying – Henry Fersko-Weiss
The Mercy Papers – Robin Romm
Finding Home: A Memoir about Love, Loss and Life's Detours – Uma Girish
Choosing To Die – Phyllis Shacter
On Living – Kerry Egan
How Not To Die – Dr. Michael Greger
When Breath Becomes Air – Paul Kalanithi
The Exit Strategy: Depriving Death of Its Strangeness – David Oliver
Stoned; A Doctor's case for Medical Marijuana – Dr. David Casarett
Overcoming the Fear of Death · Kelvin Chin
The Bright Hour – Nina Riggs
Healthy Healing – Michelle Steinke-Baumgard
Crazy Sexy Cancer – Kris Carr
Click Here when I Die – Jonathan S. Braddock
Love Your Life to Death · Yvonne Heath
The Four Agreements – Don Miguel Ruiz
LGBTQ – Inclusive Hospice and Palliative Care – Kimberly D. Acquaviva
Driving Miss Norma – Tim Bauerschmidt & Ramie Liddle
Joining Joanie – Stephanie Banks Levenston
This Chair Rocks: A Manifesto depriving Ageism – Ashton Applewhite
Confessions of a Funeral Director – Caleb Wilde
Dying Well – Ira Byock, MD
On Death and Dying – Elizabeth Kubler-Ross MD
Gone From my Sight – Barbara Karnes
Tuesdays with Morrie – Mitch Albom
Being Mortal: Medicine and What Matters in the End – Atul Gawande
The Last Lecture – Rany Pausch
Me Before You – Jojo Moyes
Final Gifts – Maggie Callanan

Advance Care Planning Resources

Death by Design – www.deathbydesign.com/resources/
My Life and Wishes – MyLifeandWishes.com
National Healthcare Decision Day – www.nhdd.org
The Conversation Project – www.theconversationproject.org
LastingMatters – www.lastingmatter.com
Begin The Conversation – www.begintheconversation.org
Aging with Dignity (Five Wishes) – www.agingwithdignity.org
National POLST Paradigm – www.polst.org
U.S. Living Will Registry – www.uslivingwillregistry.com/forms.html
My Last Soundtrack – www.mylastsoundtrack.com

Other Websites

Death by Design · www.deathbydesign.org
Nutrition Facts – www.NutritionFacts.org
One Fit Widow – www.onefitwidow.com
Kris Carr – Crazy Sexy Cancer – www.kriscarr.com
Brene Brown – www.brenebrown.com

Ted Talks

Let's talk about human composting– Katrina Spade
What makes life worth living in the face of death – Lucy Kalanithi
A burial practice that nourishes the planet – Caitlin Doughty
Before I die I want to … – Candy Chang
What really matters at the end of life – BJ Miller
Embracing death – Caleb Wide
Catch and Release – Finding Life in Death – Michael Fratkin
Palliative Care, a different voice in healthcare – Timothy Ihrig
Who's That? – Kimberly C. Paul
Am I dying? The honest answer – Matthew O'Reilly

Film/Movies

Youth In Oregon
To Joey, with Love
Consider The Conversation
Time of Death (Docu-Series Showtime)
Consider The Conversation 2
Defining Hope
How to Die in Oregon
Me Before You
Extremis

BIO

Kimberly C. Paul, BSW
Death By Design Creative Director

Applying her vast experience as a storyteller to her passion, Kimberly C. Paul is radically changing the way people face end of life. The concept of "Death by Design" is to inspire individuals and their families to create a blueprint for an inevitable journey that reflects the beauty of life and the positive destination of end of life.

After graduating from Meredith College in Raleigh, NC, Kimberly began working on the set of Saturday Night Live, casting for CBS daytime programming and freelancing for several production companies in New York City. While working in the entertainment industry, Kimberly was captivated by the creative process of developing the arc of the story. As she observed the manic rush of writing comedy skits for live television and watched daytime television actors' storylines constantly evolve, she realized she had always been interested in the story.

For the last 17 years, however, Kimberly has been telling a very different kind of story— a positive, inspiring story about designing a personal blueprint for an individual's end of life. As Vice President of Outreach and Communications for Lower Cape Fear Hospice in Wilmington, NC, she created a myriad of award-winning marketing strategies to share real stories of how hospice patients and their loved ones face the end of life journey.

As creator of the "Begin the Conversation" campaign in 2008, Kimberly was the driving force behind the program until her departure from Lower Cape Fear Hospice in 2016. "Begin the Conversation," (BTC) is a nationally recognized program encouraging the use of advance care directives with a focus on the value of conversations in advance care planning. BTC has received multiple honors and awards, including the Carolinas Healthcare Public Relations Marketing Society Silver Wallie Award (2012) for mixed media campaign and a Telly Award for best television spot (2015). In addition, the campaign won honorable mentions for Best Branding/Re-Branding and Best Social

Responsibility Campaign/Initiative in PR Daily's Nonprofit Public Relations awards competition in 2013.

Kimberly was invited to speak at TEDxAirlie in 2016. Kimberly's *Ted-Talk, Who's That?"* epitomized her passion for educating individuals about Advance Care Planning and the issues that may occur for individuals and family members if they do not prepare for end of life. During Kimberly's 18-year career in hospice care, her stories have inspired and empowered many to take action by documenting personal plans prior to the occurrence of a life-ending health crisis.

Kimberly's enthusiasm and passion to positively educate people on how to plan for end of life is evident as she shares her stories through speaking engagements, writing, videos and film. As of 2017, Kimberly is now investing 100 percent of her time to bring innovation to the death and dying industry by applying the concept of design thinking.

With a book in development for release in the upcoming months and the creation of her podcast streams for 2018, Kimberly is dedicated to providing continuous education about end of life choices with the help of leading experts in the healthcare industry and photographers, painters, authors and everyday people sharing their personal experience about love, loss, preparation and moving through grief.

"Death by Design" is an innovative, constructive and uplifting invitation to move beyond the legal paperwork and vital conversations necessary for end of life. "Death by Design" will empower you to design your death to reflect your values, your likes and even your personality. Our death, if designed, can be a beautiful experience and not just a final destination.

DEATH BY design

PODCAST

Remember... You're the Designer.

design

Overcoming the Fear

OCTOBER 2017

HEALTHY HEAL

HEALTHY HEA

THIS CHAIR ROCKS: A MAN

ASHTON APPLEWHITE

taying Connected
o Your Loved One
mentia And Beyond

NING

aanie

STON

Episode 1
Dr. Ira Byock
Original aired January 10th, 2018
"While we've strived to fight disease and maintain health, we've made it harder in many regards to die."

Episode 2
Garth Callaghan
Originally aired January 10th, 2017
Dear Emma, You can't steal second and still keep your foot on first base. - Love, Dad

Episode 3
Barbara Karnes, RN
Originally aired January 10th, 2017
"Knowledge Reduces Fear."

Episode 4
Dr. Don Schumacher, Former NHPCO President
Originally aired January 25th, 2018

Episode 5
Dr. Diane Meier, CAPC
Originally aired February 2, 2018
"The Greater Majority of young physicians and nurses do not get any training on how to talk to patients and families about their illness and what to expect."

Episode 6
Claudia Bicen
Originally aired February 9, 2018
"I wanted to create a feeling of compassion and empathy, of seeing yourself in that person. We put the elderly and the dying away, we shut them away. We've kind of given up on them. They're no longer productive...Particularly in American culture, productivity is so much at the core of what we value in people."

Episode 7
Dr. Jessica Zitter, Extreme Measures
Originally aired February 16, 2017
"Here's the reality. We're all going to die one day, and it's good to have a little bit of say in how."

Episode 8
Jeb Smith – Personal Story
Originally aired February 23, 2017
"My mom was my biggest fan."

Episode 9
Henry Fersko-Weiss, Death Doulas
Originally aired March 2, 2017
"Caring For the Dying – The Death Doula Approach to a Meaningful Death."

Episode 10
Andrew George, Photographer
Originally aired March 9, 2017
"This whole project is about life and how to live"
www.rightbeforeidie.com

Episode 11
Ginny McKinney, The Marshmallow Ranch
Originally aired March 16, 2017
"I traded my tiara for wings and a pickup truck"

Episode 12
D.S. Moss, The Adventures of Memento Mori
Originally aired March 23, 2017
"A cynics guide for learning to live by remembering to die"

Episode 13
Jon & Michelle Braddock, My Life and Wishes
Originally aired March 30, 2017
www.mylifeandwishes.com, Online platform for planning for End-of-life

Episode 14
Dr. Jack McBride, UNC Chapel Hill
Originally aired April 6, 2017
"We are going to die. We can plan for that."

Episode 15
Nathan Kottkamp, National Decisions Day
Originally aired April 13, 2017
"Nothing is certain except death and taxes." Benjamin Franklin

Episode 16
Ellen Goodman, The Conversation Project
Originally aired April 20, 2017
"I realized only after my mothers death how much easier it would have all been if I heard her voice in my ear as these decisions had to be made."

Episode 17
Barbara Bates-Sedoric, LastingMatters
Originally aired May 4, 2017
"One of the greatest gifts you can give those you love is the gift of information."

Episode 18
Deborah Kaeser
Originally aired May 11, 2017
"It was a gift to know what my mother wanted at her end of life, to support her wishes, and be with her."

Episode 19
Brenda McDonald, Personal Story
Originally aired May 18, 2017
"I want hospice care just like my mother."

Episode 20
Robin Romm, The Mercy Papers
Originally aired May 25, 2017
"If this book does land in the hands of those in the midst of a tragedy, I can tell you this: It will never leave you. And I think in the complex way of truth, that is the most comforting things."

Episode 21
Katrina Spade, The Urban Death Project
Originally aired May 25th, 2017
"Nature is really good at this dying thing."

Episode 22
Lorraine Perry, Dealing with Grief and Children
Originally aired June 1, 2017
"If I can only be with you in my dreams, then I want to sleep forever." Unknown

Episode 23
Dr. Dawn Gross, A Physician with Heart
Originally aired June 8, 2017
"The only time doctors are left with nothing more we can do is when we fail to ask."

Episode 24
Dr. BJ Miller, Palliative Care Physician
Originally aired June 15, 2017
"Parts of me died early on," he said in a recent talk. "And that's something, one way or another, we can all say. I got to redesign my life around this fact, and I tell you it has been a liberation to realize you can always find a shock of beauty or meaning in what life you have left."

Episode 25
Ben Lee, Musician and End-Of-Life Doula
Originally aired June 22, 2017
"The dying teaches me about life."

Episode 26
Shoshana Ungerleider, Co-founder of Palliative Education Fund
Originally aired June 29, 2017
"EndWell Conference is about bringing designers, creatives, and healthcare professionals together so collectively we can look at death through different eyes and change how individuals experience end of life."

Episode 27
Dr. David Grube, Compassion & Choices Medical Director
Originally aired July 6, 2017
"The more choices we have at end of life the more opportunity we will have to meet individuals where they are at end of life."

Episode 28
Andrew Eisen, Screenwriter of "Youth In Oregon"
Originally aired July 13, 2017
"The movie, Youth In Oregon, is based loosely on my family"

Episode 29
John Wadsworth, The Art of Dying Magazine
Originally aired July 20, 2017
"What is beautiful about individuals who are death aware is there's an immediate connection."

Episode 30
Uma Girish, Grief Guide and Author
Originally aired July 27, 2017
"Maybe grief is hard in America because individuals believe grief needs to be private."

Episode 31
Phyllis Shacter, Author
Originally aired August 3, 2017
"There were not a lot of resources to help us through this choice, VSED. I want others to have resources and know there are choices at end of life."

Episode 32
Tammy Beilstein & Sarah Lunsford, Let's Talk About Death
Originally aired August 10, 2017
"It's okay to laugh through death."

Episode 33
Rev. Terri Daniel
Originally aired August 17, 2017
"Like most people, I was drawn to death and dying because of a personal experience."

Episode 34
Kerry Egan, Hospice Chaplain & Author
Originally aired August 24, 2017
"Hospice Chaplains are so under utilized in the Hospice Model of care."

Episode 35
Dr. Michael Greger, Author "How Not To Die"
Originally aired August 31, 2017
"Your health is reflected in what you eat on a daily basis."

Episode 36
Dr. Karen Wyatt, End-Of-Life University
Originally aired September 7, 2017
"These are the words we were born to hear; this is the lesson we came here to learn: embrace life fully and look death in the face every day." -Father Mark

Episode 37
Dr. Lucy Kalanithi, When Breath Becomes Air
Originally aired September 14, 2017
"I began to realize that coming in such close contact with my own mortality had changed both nothing and everything. Before my cancer was diagnosed, I knew that someday I would die, but I didn't know when. After the diagnosis, I knew that someday I would die, but I didn't know when. But now I knew it acutely. The problem wasn't really a scientific one. The fact of death is unsettling. Yet there is no other way to live." -Paul Kalanithi, When Breath Becomes Air

Episode 38
Marsha Onderstijn, Animator, "The Life of Death"
Originally aired September 21, 2017
"I wanted to show the world my perspective on the Life of Death."

Episode 39
Dr. Debbie Parker-Oliver, Depriving Death of Its Strangeness
Originally aired September 28, 2017
"We teach medical students about end of life, but when they are in the field, peer pressure from older doctors leads our students away from what they were taught."

Episode 40
Dr. David Casarett, Palliative Care Physician Duke Medical Center
Originally aired October 5, 2017
"Stoned – A Doctor's Case For Medical Marijuana"

Episode 41
Charlotte Matthews, Professor UVA
Originally aired October 12, 2017
"A complete stranger told me I had breast cancer. She saved my life."

Episode 42
Dr. Tim Ihrig, Palliative Care Physician
Originally aired October 19, 2017
"It is about living throughout our final chapters of life."
and what we are." -Elisabeth Kubler-Ross

Episode 43
Dan Diaz, The Brittany Maynard Story
Originally aired November 1, 2017
"Brittany was a great person to be around – attentive, energetic, outgoing."

Episode 44
Kelvin Chin, Author, Speaker and Teacher
Originally aired October 26, 2017
"It is not the end of the physical body that should worry us. Rather, our concern must be to live while we're alive – to release our inner selves from the spiritual death that comes with living behind a facade designed to conform to external definitions of who we are."

Episode 45
Marian Grant, DNP, C-TAC: Senior Regulatory Advisor
Originally aired November 2, 2017
The Coalition to Transform Advanced Care (C-TAC) is dedicated to the ideal that all Americans with advanced illness, especially the sickest and most vulnerable, receive comprehensive, high-quality, person- and family-centered care that is consistent with their goals and values and honors their dignity.

Episode 46
Dr. Michael Fratkin, ResolutionCare
Originally aired November 9, 2017
"It's personal."

Episode 47
Michelle Steinke-Baumgard, One Fit Widow
Originally aired November 16, 2017
"When we measure things, we miss the opportunity just to love one another and support each other through life's hardest moments."

Episode 48
Kimberly C. Paul, Host of Death by Design Podcast
Originally aired November 23, 2017
"When we look at death creatively, how we face our end of life radically changes. Death is not a medical event, it is a human experience."

CPSIA information can be obtained
at www.ICGtesting.com
Printed in the USA
LVHW061416160919
631173LV00013BA/251/P